P9-DFL-401

9/11/02

MEMORY MAKERS

DISCARD

Scrapbook Journaling

made simple

Tips for telling the stories behind your photos

MEMORY MAKERS BOOKS

DENVER, COLORADO

Executive Editor Kerry Arquette   **Founders** Michele & Ron Gerbrandt

Editor Kimberly Ball
Art Director Andrea Zocchi
Craft Director Pamela Frye
Idea Editor Janetta Wieneke
Staff Artist Pam Klassen
Photographer Ken Trujillo
Contributing Photographers Marc Creedon, Christina Dooley
Designers Sylvie Abecassis, Nick Nyffeler
Contributing Writer Margaret Radford
Contributing Artists Erikia Ghumm
Editorial Support MaryJo Regier, Dena Twinem

Memory Makers® Scrapbook Journaling Made Simple

Published by Memory Makers Books, an imprint of F & W Publications, Inc.
12365 Huron Street, Suite 500, Denver, CO 80234
Phone 1-800-254-9124
First edition. Printed in the United States.

06 05 04 03 02   5 4 3 2 1

Library of Congress Cataloging-in-Publication Data

Memory makers scrapbook journaling made simple : tips for telling the stories behind your photos.
    p. cm.
    Includes bibliographical references.
    ISBN 1-892127-23-7
    1. Photographs--Conservation and restoration. 2. Scrapbook journaling. 3. Photograph albums. 4. Photograph captions. I. Title: Scrapbook journaling made simple. II. Memory makers.

TR465 .M4753 2002
745.593--dc21
                                                                                2002026589

Distributed to trade and art markets by
F & W Publications, Inc.
4700 East Galbraith Road, Cincinnati, OH 45236
Phone 1-800-289-0963

ISBN 1-892127-23-7

Memory Makers Books is the home of *Memory Makers*, the scrapbook magazine dedicated to educating and inspiring scrapbookers. To subscribe, or for more information, call 1-800-366-6465.
Visit us on the Internet at www.memorymakersmagazine.com

This Book Belongs to

We dedicate this book to all of our Memory Makers
readers, who strive to preserve their priceless
memories in pictures and in words.

14

40

Contents

7 **I**ntroduction

8   What is journaling?

9   Why you may not journal (yet)

10   Why you should journal

12 **G**etting Started

14   Spending time with your photos

15   Being a photo detective

17   Just write

18   The information every page should include

19   Leaving room for journaling

20   When you absolutely have to journal: travel, wedding, children, heritage and yourself

26 **B**eyond the Basics

28   Using descriptive words

29   List of descriptive words

30   Using active words

31   List of action words

32   Appealing to the senses

35   List of sense-related words

36   Incorporating thoughts and feelings

40   Incorporating other voices

41   Interviewing tips

42   Tools to help you journal

44   Making design and journaling work together

52 **W**hen Journaling Is Difficult

54   Overcoming writer's block

58   Writing about the hard times

62   Journaling about the photos
      you don't have

64   Adding journaling to finished pages

66   Improving your handwriting

67   Fixing journaling mistakes

68 **T**hink Outside the Box: Other Styles

70   Bullet

71   Dictionary

72   Recipe

73   Timeline

74   Postcard

75   Classified ad

76   Acrostic

77   Step-by-step

78   Fairy tale

79   Poetic

80   Found

81   Calendar

82   Newspaper

83   Perspective

84   Top-ten list

85   Correspondence

86   Rebus

87   Comic strip

88   Other styles

91   Creating book jacket bios

92   Making a memory wheel

93   Grammar guide

93   Credits, sources, bibliography

96   Index

48

74

SCHOOL NIGHTS at the Gerbrandts'

Anna (6th grade) practiced the violin. She has taken violin lessons for 3 years and is preparing for a school concert.

Daniel (1st grade) worked on a bug project. He chose to make a boll weevil. Dad and Grandpa Gerbrandt helped him with his very messy model.

Sasha (4th grade) had it easy this night. She completed her homework and wanted to play on the computer. Whoever gets done first always races for the computer.

During the week our nights are filled with the kids' homework and activities. We hardly ever reach for the TV remote Monday through Friday.

Tuesday March 19 2002

Introduction

When you look at scrapbooks or magazines, do you like to look at the pictures? Or do you read all the words? You probably tend to do one or the other. I didn't realize it before I started scrapbooking, but I am a picture person. Every page I made used to be about the photos and design; the writing was a "have to" or an afterthought that I added because people told me I was supposed to. After spending the past few years with a group of writers at *Memory Makers* magazine, the importance of the words has started to sink in. It hit home when I looked back at scrapbook pages I had made and saw that the story was missing. Sometimes I didn't even include my child's age! Since then I have worked to become a journaler. I know that if my scrapbooks are going to have an impact in the future, I need to write the story behind the photos. Now I make writing a conscious part of my design.

Whether you are a word person or a picture person, journaling has a unique set of challenges. We've created this book to help. We've come up with tips for getting started, including memory prompts and lists of descriptive and active words. We give you quick tips for improving the basics like incorporating your thoughts and feelings and appealing to the senses. We've also found ways to get you through writer's block and writing about difficult times in your life. And finally, we've included a gallery of our readers' unique styles of journaling to inspire you to break free of the journaling block. Journaling is such an important part of preserving your memories. Whether you're writing about a once-in-a-lifetime event or just about your everyday life, as I've done on the opposite page, your words will tell future generations the stories your photos can't. So get ready to grab a pen (with fade-proof pigment ink, of course) and unleash the writer in you.

Michele

Michele Gerbrandt
Founder of *Memory Makers*® magazine

What Is Journaling?

Journaling is the writing found on scrapbook pages. It takes on many forms, including simple photo captions, lists, poems, essays or stories. While the format varies, the mission is the same: to support the photos and other elements on the scrapbook pages and to say what they cannot. Journaling allows a scrapbooker to record pertinent information and convey stories. If you could be there, in person, each and every time your album is opened, you could recount the story of every page. But today's scrapbooker can't count on being on the spot each time a friend or family member wants to enjoy her albums. With archival products and scrapbooks that will last for generations to come, it is even more imperative to journal so that the stories survive with them. Journaling records in a lasting way what you say aloud about your pages. Through journaling, you'll assure that future generations will know who that sweet-faced woman in the photo is, where the picture was taken, why and when. Journaling is your voice, your artistic statement and your interpretation of the events that make up your world.

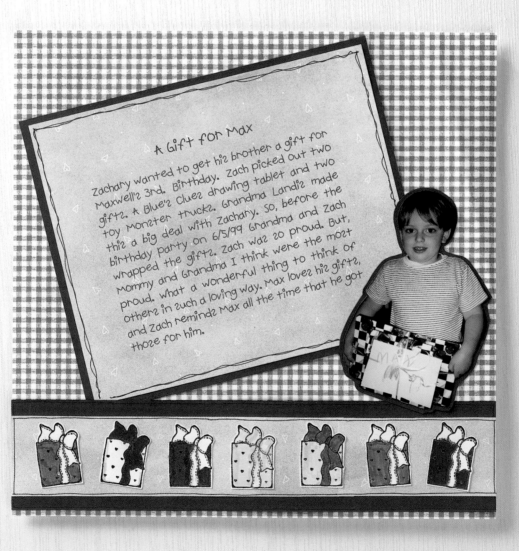

A Gift for Max

Zachary wanted to get his brother a gift for Maxwell's 3rd. Birthday. Zach picked out two gifts. A Blue's Clues drawing tablet and two toy Monster trucks. Grandma Landis made this a big deal with Zachary. So, before the birthday party on 6/5/99 Grandma and Zach wrapped the gifts. Zach was so proud. But, Mommy and Grandma I think were the most proud. What a wonderful thing to think of others in such a loving way. Max loves his gifts, and Zach reminds Max all the time that he got those for him.

Journaling tells the story behind your photos. Michele Rank of Cerritos, California, captured a priceless childhood memory in just one short paragraph. Product information for all pages in this book can be found in on pages 94, 95 & 96.

Why You May Not Journal (Yet)

You may view journaling as a necessary evil. You reluctantly set pen to paper now and then out of a vague sense of duty. You may journal religiously but without substance—abbreviating stories whenever it's convenient. You may enjoy journaling "normal" pages but freeze when it comes to describing special events or emotional situations. You may refuse to journal at all. If you've lost (or never had) enthusiasm for journaling, it's probably because:

- You don't feel you have anything interesting to say.
- You hate your handwriting.
- You are afraid of making a mistake that will ruin your page.
- You prefer to focus on the page design.
- You lack information about the photo and don't know how to find it.
- You lack photos and feel uncomfortable writing about an event without them.
- You are convinced you don't write well.
- You fail to leave journaling space on your pages and then don't know where to write.
- You don't know how to write about a painful event.
- You don't know how to begin.
- You're afraid you'll say too much or too little.
- You "just can't find the time."
- You truly don't believe that journaling is important.

Why You Should Journal

Writing—and reading what others have written—are the closest things to time travel humanity may ever know. Consider the wonder of it: Perhaps 8,000 years ago a man jotted a note on clay or papyrus. Millennia later the message is found and the thoughts of that long-ago scribe are as clear to you today as they were the day he wrote them.

Like writing, scrapbooking preserves moments in time. You spend time and effort collecting and presenting your photos and memorabilia so that future generations will have a visual record of your life and times. Isn't it worth it to complete that record with journaling? Yes, a picture is worth a thousand words, but those "thousand words" rarely communicate the whole story. Journaling adds context and substance to your scrapbook pages and magnifies the power of your photos. Choose your words carefully, as you do the photos you include on your spreads. The right words complete the story, encapsulating an intact moment, whole and alive, for future generations.

By writing down her friends' wedding vows, Yvonne Laura Torres of Miami, Florida, ensured they would be preserved for years to come.

*My Grandmother
(Margaret Ellen Ritchey)
was a living monument to
fortitude and strength. She
survived fire, polio and
heartbreak as a child...Her
belief that hardships were
to be overcome rather than
resented was evident in
every aspect of her life...*

Grandma w/ Mom 1950/51

My Grandmother (Margaret Ellen Ritchey) was a living monument to fortitude and strength. She survived fire, polio and heartbreak as a child and, as a woman, she suffered from nearly crippling arthritis. Her belief that hardships were to be overcome rather than resented was evident in every aspect of her life—from her sweet smile to extravagant Christmas dinners, to an immaculate home and lovely, garden-of-a yard.

The most valuable gifts she gave me were lessons (the value of tradition, that there's nothing more valuable than a loving family and the meaning of "right") and memories (memories of love and autumn leaves and quiet talks and birthdays shared). Good lessons and good memories from a truly good woman. I feel that if I live a life that she would be proud of, I've accomplished a great deal. Thank you Grandma

Poppy and Grandma And the Sisters Lorri, Jane Sue (Mom) and Kathy (L to R) Standing

Nicole Gartland of Portland, Oregon, recorded fond memories of her grandmother. Without Nicole's reflections, the essence of this loving woman may have disappeared forever.

Missy Lori
L. Nicole Chris
Chandi Valerie
Natalie Jacob G. Wesley Katie Cassie Jo
Christie Jacki DanJi
Holly Vicky Zachard
Shane Jacob

This stone wall represents each of the Grand and Great-Grand Children while leaving plenty of room for the ones that aren't here yet.

 Getting Started

There's an old saying: "Write what you know." When you write what you know, the words flow more easily. That's good news for you as a scrapbooker. In your scrapbook, you write about the things that are most important in your life—your heritage, your class reunion, your children's birthdays. If you find even writing about these subjects difficult, it may be because you lack the confidence to let the words that are in your head and heart become part of the paper. If you are convinced that writing is a talent shared by few, visit your local library or bookstore. The hundreds of thousands of books and magazines on the shelves are testimony to the fact that writing is not a rare gift. It is a skill that most of us can acquire. And unlike the authors of those books and magazines, you don't have the burden of writing to complete strangers. You have stories to tell that your particular readers will find compelling—stories about you and them and the times you share. You have a captive audience thirsting for the words you set down. Quench their thirst.

Spending Time With Your Photos

Something has inspired you to begin scrapbooking. Perhaps it is photos or memorabilia from an experience that's very important to you. Those mementos, along with journaling, will be the backbone of your scrapbook page. Pull out those photos. Look through them, taking notes as you recall their histories. Jot down pertinent information on sticky notes or in a notebook. Note times, dates, names of people, locations, events. Once you have the basic information down, flesh out the journaling details by asking a friend or family member to sit with you while you talk about the experience. Allow the photos to guide you as you speak, but don't be constrained by what they show. If you remember an anecdote that isn't represented by the photos, share it. While you're speaking, listen to yourself. Those stories, the ones that rise to the top to be shared out loud, are the ones worth writing down in your scrapbook.

During the summer of 2000 Tony and Amanda went camping at Red Feather Lakes several times. She loved staying in our travel trailer. Everything was an adventure to our very busy little girl and our dogs, Kolob and Abby. At 2½, Amanda learned to fish, but mostly liked to play in the water and mud. The only down side to these trips were no campfires, because of the extreme fire hazard and the nightly visits of the bears. We were glad we had a trailer!

CAMPING

The trailer is old, but very warm and comfortable

Pam Klassen of Westminster, Colorado, journaled about her daughter Amanda's camping fun, including events that happened both in front of the camera and behind the scenes.

Being a photo detective

Solving the riddle of an old photo is a skill and an art. Before you can figure out who the subject is, you may need to find out where and when the photo was taken. Begin by asking older family members what they know about the photo. Then slip on your cotton gloves and pick up your magnifying glass. Hairstyles, hemlines and other fashions, landmarks, newspapers and year-specific products such as cars will help you determine a time frame during which the photo was taken. Look for a photographer's mark or signature.

The physical nature of the photograph (metal, tin, paper, etc.) provides clues as well. Dedicate a notebook to keeping track of your research and consult the guides to historical photos available at your library and bookstore.

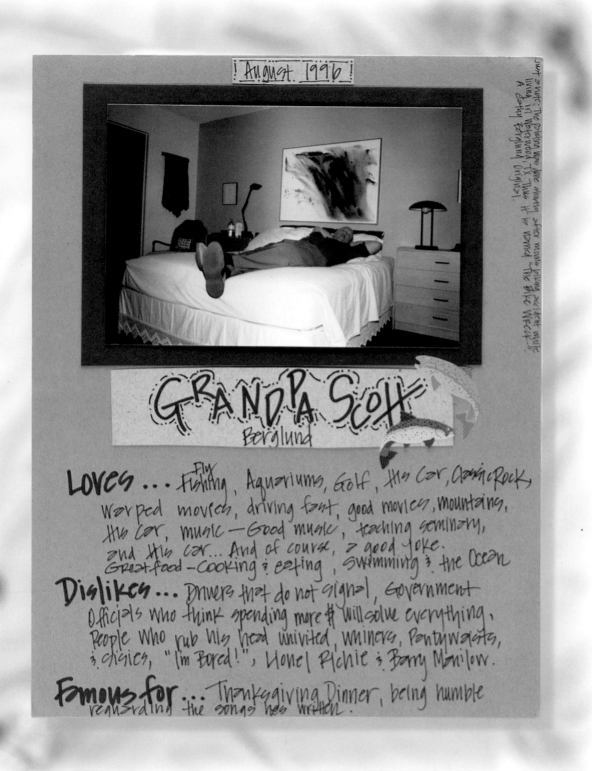

August 1996

GRANDPA SCOTT
Berglund

LOVES ... Fly Fishing, Aquariums, Golf, His Car, Classic Rock, warped movies, driving fast, good movies, mountains, His Car, music—Good music, teaching seminary, and His car... And of course, a good joke. Great food—Cooking & eating, swimming & the Ocean

Dislikes ... Drivers that do not signal, Government Officials who think spending more $ will solve everything, People who rub his head uninvited, whiners, Pantywaists, & dishes, "I'm Bored!", Lionel Richie & Barry Manilow.

Famous for ... Thanksgiving Dinner, being humble regarding the songs he's written.

Kim Bowler, of Gunlock, Utah shared her warm feelings about her stepfather in this scrapbook page. She says "Grandpa Scott" who has been in the military police, a songwriter and in medical risk management is quite a character and she wanted to create a page that would allow her children to know him better.

Just Write

Don't worry about writing right. Just write! Forget all those school lectures about sentence structure, handwriting and punctuation. Get out your nicest pen and paper or flex your finger muscles on the keyboard. Wade into your stream of consciousness. Write what you're thinking at this exact moment. Describe the groceries you need to buy. Record an interesting conversation you had with the bank teller. Pretend as though you're writing a letter to a good friend. Tell her about your day. Don't know how to write it? List what you would write about if you could. In writing, as in all art, it is the sincerity that carries the song, the passion that makes others take notice. So don't edit your thoughts or your work. Don't correct. Don't worry about how it sounds. Just write.

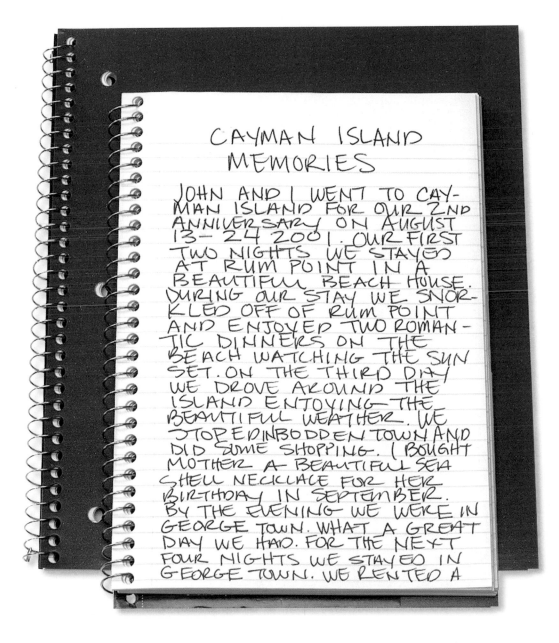

The Information Every Page Should Include

To know what information is absolutely essential, think about what those who will read your journaling will want to know. Pull out an old album or check out a photo-heavy historical book from your library. Cover the captions. Now study the pictures. What questions come to mind? Most likely they are the "five W's and the H." That's Who, What, When, Where, Why and How. As in, who and what are in the photo, when and where was it taken, why did someone want to remember this moment and how did this moment come about? These questions and their answers form the basis of good journaling. Whether you choose to answer them in list form or write flowing sentences, take the time to set down these basic facts for each photo on your scrapbook pages.

Journaling doesn't have to be fancy or extensive, and it certainly doesn't have to interfere with the design of your page. Lori Pieper of C-Thru Ruler Company captured the who, what, when and where of a wedding portrait in two simple ovals that echo the photo frame.

Leaving room for journaling

It is easier to plan for journaling in the design of your pages than to retrofit journaling onto an existing page. To ensure you have enough space for your words, consider creating a sketch of your page prior to beginning the actual layout. The sketch will serve as a crude map of your page—one that takes into account space for photos, memorabilia and journaling.

Simply pencil in areas designated for visuals and text. This is your chance to make changes large and small before permanent ink and adhesives are even at the table with you. Once you're satisfied, refer to the sketch as you begin to set the elements on your page.

When You Absolutely Have to Journal

It is said that at life's end, few look back and wish they had spent more time at work. We are more likely to reflect on the occasions spent with loved ones, with the world around us and with our own thoughts and wish we had reveled in more of the same. We reflect upon a handful of most treasured moments, each a turning point in life. These events are the focus of much of our picture-taking and should be the focus of much of our journaling. If you journal about nothing else, you must write about your travels, your wedding, the birth and growth of your children, and your family history and heritage. But also set aside time to journal about your own unique personality. These are the thoughts and moments that define who you are as an individual. Sharing them with others is truly a gift beyond words.

Travel

When you finally take that once-in-a-lifetime trip, you'll experience things you only dreamed about. The sights can be captured with your camera but the sounds, tastes and smells, as well as the way you felt about them, can only be recorded through journaling. So be sure to pack pens and paper so you can take notes as events unfold, or set aside time to write about your travels as soon as you get back home.

Day 1 – Friday
We awoke at 3:00 a.m. for a very early flight at 5:30 for our trip to St. Croix. After what seemed like a very long day, we arrived in St. Croix at 2:00 p.m. and felt the wonderful soft, warm Caribbean air as soon as we walked off the plane. A driver picked us up to take us to the car rental shop near Christiansted, then we drove the incredible drive to Carambola Beach Resort. What an amazing view as we came around the bend overlooking Davis Bay and Carambola. The Carambola is an older, casual resort, built by Laurance Rockefeller on the side of a hill right on the beach.

We got unpacked quickly and headed right out to the beach, where I snorkeled in rough surf for a brief time. We both fell asleep on the beach while relaxing after our long day! Dinner was the Pirate's Buffet in the Saman/Mahogany Room main restaurant. The food was terrific. Finally, exhausted, but happy, we went back to our room and fell asleep.

Day 2 – Saturday
We started out very slowly, making coffee and sitting on our screened in veranda. We then went to breakfast in the Saman room, where we enjoyed a beautiful view of the ocean. We went to the dive shop on site and made arrangements for a shore dive. Thankfully, a divemaster named Jeff, heard our conversation, and, what incredible luck – he joined us! The surf was rough again, so we submerged in about eight feet of water. The dive ran along the wall and was really very nice.

In the afternoon, we went into town to get groceries, driving on The Beast, a twisting, turning, climbing road that goes through the heart of St. Croix. We came back and had a nice dinner at the Flamboyant Lounge, a little place in the resort that served great food. We ended the evening with a rousing game of gin rummy –our usual vacation past time!

Day 3 – Sunday
We had another slow, easy morning, getting ready for our first boat dives with Anchor Dive. The first dive was on a wall and we went to 68 feet! After a rest back at their Salt River dive shop, our second dive was following a pipeline that fed the local shrimp hatchery until it was devastated by Hurricane Hugo. The dive was fantastic. We saw a HUGE lobster and many, colorful fish.

At night, we ate at the Flamboyant Lounge again and watched a truly lovely sunset. We then took a walk around the grounds, listening to the tree toads and looking for the tennis courts. The lighted courts were waiting for us – for another day perhaps. We walked along the beach and sat in a hammock watching the moon and the ocean. What an enchanting place!

Day 4– Monday
We drove to Christiansted in the morning and walked around the historic Danish town. The shops were terrific, lined up along a beautiful boardwalk around the bay. We had lunch at a great little second floor restaurant called Tivoli Garden that had a great view of Galleon Bay. We spent some more time in the shops and then explored Fort Christianvaern, the best-preserved Danish fort in the West Indies.

We drove part way back to Carambola to Cane Bay and stopped to watch the sunset at Boz's Beach Bar. We were lucky enough to get seats overlooking the ocean, so we stayed and had dinner. Life just doesn't get much better!

Sandi Parrish of Grand Rapids, Michigan, documented the highlights of her trip to St. Croix in a two-page spread accented with colorful florals. If you have many details to share, consider devoting a whole page or spread to journaling.

Day 5 – Tuesday
We started out with the breakfast buffet at Carambola, then drove to Salt River Bay (where Columbus landed in 1493) for another day of diving with Anchor Dive. We started with an 80' dive on the East Wall! Amazing! We saw a coral crab, arrow crab, black coral and many beautiful and colorful fish. We came back to their dive shop in Salt River for our surface interval and chatted with the other divers including Dave from Rochester and Jeff, the divemaster that we joined for the shore dive earlier in the week. We also met Julie, a young student from Calgary.

The afternoon dive was in 60' at Gentle Winds. It was a nice, easy "spur and groove" dive and, again, saw many beautiful, colorful fish. After diving, we had dinner at The Waves, right at sunset on the beach. It could not have been more lovely.

Day 6 – Wednesday
We drove into Christiansted for a day sail to Buck Island. We met two great couples, Dave (from diving the day before) and his wife Deborah, and Gloria and Allen from London. Tommy, our captain, gave us a terrific 6-mile sail from the harbor at Christiansted to Buck Island on the Trimaran, Trine. We snorkeled for an hour around the reef, which was extensively damaged by Hurricane Hugo. There were huge elkhorn coral formations and lots of fish – including a HUGE school of blue tangs, very large snappers, trumpet fish and a large barracuda.

We had lunch on the beach at Buck Island, named one of the 10 best in the world by National Geographic. After paddling around in the water, we joined Tommy for the ride back to Christiansted. We met everyone in the bar for a leisurely drink, then headed back to the resort for a refreshing dip in the pool at Carambola. Later, we were joined by Divemaster Jeff and his wife Mary at the "Off the Wall" where we had a nice, casual dinner and listened to a great jazz combo. The sunset was beautiful and the company just right!

Day 7 – Thursday
We went diving with Anchor Dive and there was only three of us with the Divemaster, Gary. We dove the East Wall again and saw barracuda and a scorpionfish. The water was kind of cloudy, which was interesting, but it was still a very nice dive. After our surface interval, we went to Pinellas, and saw two enormous southern stingrays hiding under the sand. It was also the first day using the underwater camera, so that was interesting.

After diving, we stopped at Columbus Cove for drinks and snacks, then drove to Off The Wall for the sunset and burgers. Better burgers, in Paradise, were never made. We saw Jeff and Mary and said goodbye to them. Back at the resort, I took a beautiful and relaxing swim, all alone, in the pool. What a great day!

Day 8 – Last day
We drove into Christiansted, which was very busy from the upcoming Half Ironman. Competitors were everywhere. We went to the St. Croix Aquarium and then went to lunch at Rumrunner, right on the bay. After a little shopping, we drove back to Carambola and drove around the golf course villas. Ahhh☐one can dream. We drove back to Carambola for a quick swim before packing.

We went to the beach for the last sunset and then had dinner at the Pirate's Buffet. We came full circle – we started and ended at the Pirate's buffet. What an incredible place and what a terrific trip!

- Why did you choose to visit that particular place?
- How did you feel on the way to your destination?
- What did you wish you had brought with you?
- What were the most exciting, the scariest and most moving things that happened on your trip?
- What sounds, smells, tastes, sights and feelings will you always associate with that place?
- How were the people you met on your trip the same as or different from you?
- Was a language barrier ever a problem? How did you overcome it?
- Did you make any cultural faux pas?

- Who did you meet that had the greatest impact on your trip?
- Were you homesick?
- What did you miss most while away from home?
- What did you learn about yourself while traveling?
- How did you feel on your way home?
- In hindsight, are you glad you went?
- What do you wish you had done differently?
- Would you go back if you had the chance?
- Who from your trip, if anyone, do you stay in touch with?
- What advice would you give people traveling to the same locale?

Wedding

You will remember the excitement of your wedding for the rest of your life. But many of the little details that make up the big event can easily be forgotten amidst the hustle and bustle of your honeymoon and setting up house. So make a vow to set aside all those thank-you notes that must be written and spend some time journaling about your wedding and the special events surrounding it.

- What did your friends and family do to keep you calm—or stress you out?
- What were the best and worst pieces of marital advice you received?
- Who was in the bridal party, and why were they chosen?
- How did you feel the night before the ceremony?
- What did you do to combat wedding-day jitters?
- How did you fulfill the requirements of "something old, something new, something borrowed and something blue"?
- How did you feel ten minutes before the ceremony? During the ceremony?
- Who cried the hardest at the ceremony?
- Did you add any special traditions to the ceremony?
- What went right and what went wrong?
- To whom were you the most grateful for coming?
- What was the funniest thing that happened on your wedding day?
- Did your spouse do anything surprising?
- What was the most difficult part of getting married?
- Why did you pick your first dance song?
- What were the best and worst presents you received?
- When did you first refer to your spouse as your husband or wife? How did it feel?

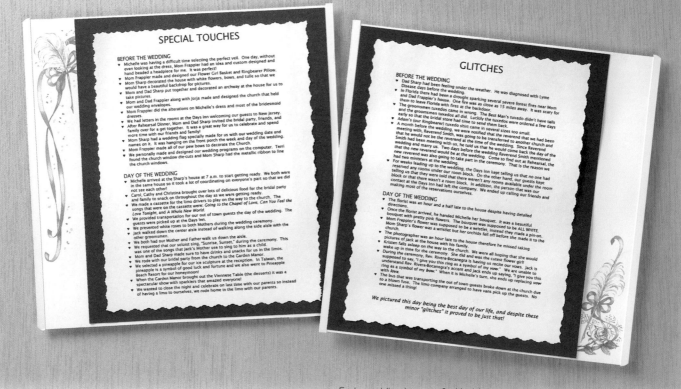

Each wedding is one of a kind; be sure to record the details that made yours unique. Michelle Sharp of Orlando, Florida, wrote down the highs and lows of the day she got hitched.

She's red when she's righteous "no, that's mine..." Cayra is peaceful when she's purple.

Using color as her uniting theme, Deidre Tansey of Smithers, BC, Canada, recorded the many moods of her daughter's precious toddler years.

Children

With the birth of a child your life changes forever, and it continues to change as the years cycle by. Before you know it, your "baby" is an independent teenager, and the memory of those first baby steps are easily forgotten as he strides on toward adulthood. Record all the special moments in your scrapbooks before they fade. Document the love you poured into parenting and the love that your child returned ten times over.

- What was your reaction when you found out you were going to be a parent?
- How did you feel the first time you held your child?
- What was your child's first word?
- How did you feel when he started kindergarten?
- When were you most afraid for your child?
- What did you and your child disagree about most often?
- How did you teach your child about his heritage?
- What are your greatest hopes for your child?
- What do you wish you could have given your child that you could not?
- How did your parents influence the way you brought up your child?
- What did you do as a parent that you swore you would never do?
- What moment in your child's life makes you the most proud?
- What personality traits does your child share with you? With your spouse?
- What family member does your child most resemble?
- What are your child's greatest strengths and weaknesses?
- What are your child's nicknames, and how did he get them?

Heritage

An old photograph can be a window to the past that reveals an expanse of information about your family history. Ensure that future generations understand the importance of these treasures by showcasing them in scrapbooks. Take the time to research a bit about those in the pictures. The personal information you include on your pages can breathe life into old portraits. Journaled descriptions and stories turn two-dimensional images into compelling relatives.

- Who is in the photo?
- When and where was the photo taken?
- Who took the photo and why?
- What is happening in the photo?
- What do you know about this person's life?
- Who were his parents and what did they do professionally?
- What was his religion?
- When and where was he born?
- Where did he grow up?
- Did he have any special interests or hobbies?
- What was his profession?
- What happened historically during his life that impacted its direction?
- How do you and others remember and describe this person?
- If you know nothing about this person, what do you imagine his life was like?
- What are the major differences between life then and life now?
- What feelings does this photo evoke in you?

Laurie Capener of Providence, Utah, revives the groovy days of the '60s and '70s with pieces of old advertisements, heritage photos and journaling about the trends of the time.

Lisa R. Trent of Moorpark, California, decided to make a journaling album to record important memories of her life for which she didn't have photos. If you hesitate to include private thoughts and memories in your family scrapbook, consider creating your own personal journaling scrapbook.

Q: Tell about your memories of a slumber party or sleepover.

9/28/99:

Most of the sleepovers we had as kids were at Grandma Thera's house. All of the cousins: Tirza, myself, Kim, Kelly, Heather, Heather's good friend Blake, and sometimes Grace and Laura, would go down to Grandma Thera's house frequently and have a big sleepover. We'd have all our sleeping bags piled on the living room floor. I actually don't remember a lot of the specifics about the sleepovers, just that of a general feeling of nostalgia, and sadness that we don't get together as frequently anymore. I do remember talking and watching home movies when we were there. I also remember staying over at Tina Fosnight's house in about 6th grade... it was the first time I ever stayed up all night telling ghost stories. I don't know any, but I had fun... and was maybe a little scared... listening to other people's versions of their ghost stories. Tina's living room was perfect for that. It had this incredibly huge vaulted ceiling... it must have been 40 feet tall. I remember that Janet Butterfield was there, and myself; I'm not sure if anyone else was.

I also used to stay at Felicia's house, when she was living with her aunt Mary. For a few years, when we were between about 9 & 12, we were pretty inseparable. She would stay at our place, too. I remember we would fight for the covers. I would sleep with my body under the covers edge, so she couldn't get them!! ☺

Yourself

As the family chronicler, you may feel too busy recording the lives of others to think about recording your own activities. But your dedication will have future generations wondering who was behind the camera. Don't let that happen. Make a point to regularly step into the picture and include interesting information about yourself when journaling. Don't hold back. These scrapbook pages are the footprints in history that you'll leave behind.

- How did you get your name?
- What are your religious beliefs?
- What are your greatest accomplishments?
- What is your motto?
- Why do you scrapbook?
- How is your life different than you imagined it would be?
- What are your favorite and least favorite things?

- What did you want to be when you grew up?
- What do you do professionally? How did you choose your career?
- What are your nicknames? Who gave them to you and why?
- What do you like about yourself and what would you change if you could?
- How did your upbringing influence the person you became?
- Who is your hero and why? Has it changed over the years?
- How would your friends and family describe you?
- What was the best piece of advice you ever received?
- What important lesson have you learned that you'd like to pass on?

OUR FAMILY

THESE PHOTOS
REMIND ME OF HOW FAST
MY CHILDREN ARE GROWING, AND
HOW PROUD THEY MAKE ME EVERYDAY.
I'M SO GLAD WE TOOK THE TIME
TO TAKE THESE PORTRAITS.

DECEMBER 2001

Beyond the Basics

"Find what gave you emotion;

what the action was that gave

you excitement. Then write it down,

making it clear so that the

reader can see it, too."

-Ernest Hemingway,

fiction writer, playwright and poet

Deciding to journal is the first step on a writing path you will travel throughout your life. Think of everything you've journaled so far as your "rough drafts," your glorious first tries. With your next strides forward, you will explore ways to use words so they capture the essence of your experiences. You'll learn to give your words depth, color, movement and a life of their own. You'll weave words so they describe senses: how things feel, taste, smell and sound. Just as important, the habit of writing empowers you to record the thoughts and feelings you and others experience. If you wish, your journaling can reflect a wide range of emotions—excitement, enthusiasm, even sadness. The only thing you'll need to take on this trip is a pen, paper and a willingness to open yourself up to new experiences. In journaling, you reveal so much about your topic... and about yourself.

Using Descriptive Words

Every writer shoulders a toolbox brimming with tools that add depth and color to their work. One important tool is descriptive words. You already use nouns—words for people, places and things. And you know adjectives—words that describe those things. Yet in writing you may not choose the same meaningful nouns and adjectives you would in conversation. With that in mind, revisit a recent example of your journaling. What could be more expressive? A trip becomes an odyssey. The sky isn't just blue; it's sapphire blue. Specific details are descriptive, too. It's easy to picture a man who is 6'6", but what does "tall" look like? Your mission isn't to use all the tools, by the way. The key is using the right tool for the job.

> Thanksgiving dinner was great this year. Mom made a big turkey, and everyone ate a lot. The table setting was very pretty. We all had a good time.

> Thanksgiving dinner was truly a feast this year. Mom made a 20-pound turkey, and the ten of us very nearly finished it off. Dad called the gorgeous table setting a masterpiece. By the end of the night, we all felt full, satisfied and very thankful.

Compare these two journaling blocks. The one on the bottom uses more descriptive nouns, such as "feast" instead of "dinner" and "masterpiece" to describe the setting. A 20-pound turkey is easier to picture than a turkey that's only described as "big." And the last sentence gives a much richer account of the jovial feelings than "good time."

List of descriptive words

Keep your descriptions of people, places and things fresh with exciting adjectives. Forgo those over-used words that add little to your journaling and choose alternatives that pack more punch. A dictionary or thesaurus offers thousands of options, or find "amazing," "unique" words in the list below.

abominable	feral	one-of-a-kind
abundant	ferocious	ordinary
adorable	flagrant	oppressive
aggressive	flawless	ornery
amazing	foremost	outmoded
ambivalent	formidable	petulant
animated	frumpy	pitiable
astounding	fussy	placid
bedraggled	gigantic	poignant
befuddled	glossy	potent
bemused	goofy	priceless
bewitching	huge	prissy
bittersweet	humble	pure
blatant	husky	quirky
boisterous	hysterical	radiant
bombastic	idiosyncratic	rambunctious
breath-taking	imaginative	rare
bright	immaculate	reprehensible
callow	influential	routine
candescent	intrigued	rowdy
carefree	invariable	sensational
catty	invincible	shallow
cherished	jerky	sickening
clear	juicy	significant
coarse	killjoy	spellbinding
commendable	laudatory	stupendous
complex	leading	sturdy
dainty	loved	successful
dappled	ludicrous	symmetrical
decadent	lustrous	tangy
delicate	magical	threadbare
disastrous	magnetic	toutable
distinctive	magnificent	translucent
diverse	massive	turgid
eccentric	mind-boggling	unconventional
enterprising	mouth-watering	unexpected
entertaining	muscular	unfamiliar
ethereal	mysterious	uproarious
excessive	nasal	vain
existing	nasty	vaporish
exquisite	nimble	vivid

Using Active Words

Verbs and adverbs breathe life and movement into your writing. If nouns and adjectives represent a comic strip, verbs and adverbs are like an animated film. Strong, descriptive verbs and adverbs bellow rather than whisper. You could describe your seaside adventure by writing "The seagulls flew in for scraps," but it would read more vibrantly if you wrote "The gulls dove hungrily for scraps."

Typically verbs are strongest when used in the active voice. "The gulls ate the scraps" is much stronger than "The scraps were eaten by the gulls." When writing in the active voice, the person or thing doing the action is the subject of the sentence. To keep the active voice moving, avoid beginning sentences with phrases like "There were ..." Make a habit of looking for those pesky "weres" that sneak into your sentences; prune them off and get right to the action.

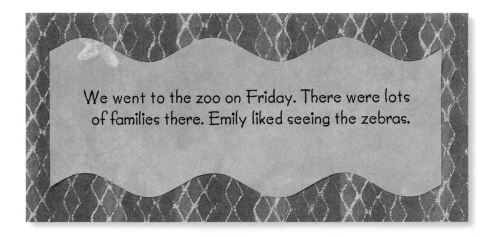

We went to the zoo on Friday. There were lots of families there. Emily liked seeing the zebras.

On Friday, we drove out to the zoo. Crowds of people milled around, oohing and ahhing at all the different animals. When we walked by the zebra pen, Emily laughed out loud. We could hardly pull her away.

The journaling on the lower block paints a much more active picture. The reader knows not only about the abundance of people at the zoo but also what they were doing. She understands Emily's actions and also gleans her attitude. Showing, rather than telling, can immediately pump up the action in your journaling.

List of action words

Just the right "action" word will jazz up your journaling. The next time you're tempted to use an old standby verb such as "was," "went" or "said," substitute a word with more zing. The right verb can add spark to less lively subjects and make reading more interesting.

ambled	heaved	promenaded
aspired	heralded	questioned
astounded	hobbled	queried
beguiled	hopped	raced
bewildered	hurled	rammed
blathered	imparted	ran
bloomed	impinged	rocketed
bounced	implied	routed
burned	jilted	ruminated
cajoled	jogged	ruptured
cantered	juggled	sang
capered	jumped	sauntered
caterwauled	junked	shouted
crawled	keeled over	shoved
croaked	kibitzed	shrugged
danced	kiboshed	shuffled
darted	lumbered	skipped
dashed	lunged	slithered
diminished	luxuriated	sparkled
dissipated	magnified	sprinted
distracted	maligned	sprouted
diverged	meandered	strolled
emerged	migrated	surged
engaged	moseyed	swayed
ensured	negotiated	swelled
entreated	niggled	testified
envisioned	nuzzled	threw
exalted	orated	tossed
extrapolated	outpoured	touted
fabricated	overtook	trotted
flew	pandered	twinkled
flinched	panicked	vaporized
flourished	performed	vouched
flowed	pierced	waggled
flung	played	walked
frolicked	plodded	wandered
fuddled	poked	whispered
fumed	postured	wiggled
galloped	pounced	yee-hawed
gamboled	pranced	yelled
gleamed	prodded	yodeled

Mom practiced 3 times a day for 3 weeks.
Mom's lip got big and strong.

Appealing to the Senses

We experience the world largely through sight, sound, touch, smell and taste, yet we often forget how powerfully our memories are entwined with those senses. A sweet whiff of freesia in the air may resurrect the feeling of the wedding bouquet in your grasp. A snippet of a brassy oldie on the radio conjures memories of your parents dancing around the kitchen. Good writing calls upon all of the senses in order to bring a scene to life. It's often easiest to write how something or someone looks, but the smells, tastes, textures and sounds that make up events will transport your reader into the memory more fully. So make a conscious effort to record the soft bounce of your grandmother's featherbed or the lilting twitter of a bird, and your writing will become as rich as homemade dumplings.

The sounds of the shofar carry on ancient Hebrew liturgical rituals. By including descriptions of the sounds, Kimberly Trachtman of Sharpsville, Pennsylvania, preserved an important Rosh Hashanah tradition for her family.

GRANDPA RUDY WITH MOM 1938

Grandpa Rudy loved growing tomatoes. He called them "God's jewels in the earth." Year after year, his tomatoes were fat, juicy and delicious. The secret, he said, was to water them in the dark - once before dawn and again after sunset.

Grandpa Rudy's Tomato Sauce
(Makes 4-6 cups)

1 T. olive oil
2 ounces pork butt, diced
3 cloves of garlic minced
1 onion, diced
1 green bell pepper, diced
8-10 fresh tomatoes, peeled and chopped
2 T. tomato paste
1 cup red wine
1 cup water
½ cup fresh basil, chopped
1 t. sugar
¼ t. salt
¼ t. pepper

Brown pork and garlic in oil. Add onion and bell pepper. Cook until onions are translucent. Add remaining ingredients. Stir well and bring to a boil. Simmer uncovered for about two hours, or until sauce is thickened.

Including a family recipe in a scrapbook preserves tasty traditions and well-guarded secret ingredients. Add a photo of the chef, as artist Erikia Ghumm of Brighton, Colorado, has done in this page featuring Kathy Steligo of San Carlos, California, and her father.

The best part of picking the peaches is that you also get to EAT the peaches! They were amazing!...Life doesn't get much better for a little girl!

eckerts farm

We could feel the humidity in the air as soon as we got out of the car. The air is so thick in St. Louis during the summer you can almost cut it with a knife.
Fresh peaches still have soft fuzz all over them that should be removed before eating. It's easy to have fuzz all over your hands and if you're not careful you can get it on your body and it will make you itch all over!

As we approached the orchard you could smell the sweet scent of peaches filling the air. Every time you picked a peach off the tree you would put your little nose up to it and sniff several times to make sure it was good.

Everywhere we looked were peach trees filled with ripe peaches just waiting to be picked. There must have been thousands of trees and some of the really good peaches were all the way at the top. Daddy carried you on his shoulder so that you could get a birds eye view.

The best part of picking the peaches is that you also get to EAT the peaches! They were amazing! Fresh, ripe, sweet, and juicy peaches right off the tree—they tasted so yummy! Life doesn't get much better for a little girl!

While we were filling our crates with peaches you could hear other people snapping their own peaches off the trees and children running up and down the rows yelling with excitement when they found a cluster of ripe peaches.

August 4, 2000

Brandi Ginn of Lafayette, Colorado, calls up all five senses on her peach-picking page. She describes the look of the peach orchard, the sweet scent and fuzzy texture of the fruit, the sound they made falling from the limbs and their juicy taste.

List of sense-related words

Use this list to help you add sensual detail to your journaling. Your photos show others what you saw through the lens of your camera, but these and other great "zesty," "savory" words will lend insight into the smells, tastes, sounds and textures that accompanied the events.

SMELLS

acidic
aromatic
camphoric
fetid
flowery
foul
fragrant
fresh
funky
heady
musky
musty
nasty
noxious
perfumed
piney
pungent
rancid
savory
smelly
stinky
stuffy
sweet

TASTES

acidic
biting
bitter
brackish
briny
delectable
delicious
dry
flavorful
fruity
full-bodied

gamy
gross
juicy
peppery
pickled
rank
rich
salty
savory
sharp
sour
spicy
succulent
sugary
sweet
syrupy
tangy
tart
zesty
zingy

SOUNDS

bang
blare
bleat
bray
brogue
caterwaul
chime
chirp
chortle
chuckle
clash
croak
croon
crunch
ding

drone
fizz
grind
groan
gulp
gurgle
hoot
howl
jangle
jingle
keen
knock
ping
plop
prattle
rap
rasp
rattle
roar
rumble
rustle
sizzle
slam
slap
slurp
snarl
strum
tap
thud
thunk
tinkle
trill
twang
warble
whack
whine
whistle
yodel

TOUCH

biting
bristly
bumpy
burning
bushy
caressable
cottony
damp
downy
feathery
frosty
furry
fuzzy
gnarled
greasy
hairy
knobbed
knotted
leathery
lumpy
oily
puffy
ribbed
rigid
rough
rubbery
sandy
sharp
slimy
smooth
soapy
sticky
textured
tough
velvety
wet

Incorporating Thoughts and Feelings

A writer uses words much as a sculptor uses a chisel—to give concepts shape. Yet you have nothing without the underlying marble, your thoughts and feelings. Your strongest feelings are likely tied to the most important events of your time—be it your wedding or news that a national leader has been assassinated. If life is literature, these are the classics, the moments that endure and serve as milestones in your life. Writing about these events is imperative. When doing so, choose language that is simple and clear and a style that reinforces the power of the occasion without overshadowing it. Remember, no writer is obligated to share information deemed too private. Open the door to your heart slowly, but don't shy away from the intensity of your feelings in your journaling because those emotions reveal your humanity to your readers. Without them, your memories are reduced to nothing more than historical facts.

Life-changing events evoke strong emotions, but smaller, everyday happenings can strike the heart equally deeply. For Tami Mayberry of Lonedell, Missouri, a simple comparison between father and son jolted an awareness of her son's quick growth and change.

The Simple Things

Sometimes the most simple things in life are worth remembering. One day Ryan went in Auto Zone with David. When they came out there he was walking beside his Dad. He looked so tiny but at the same time made me realize how big he is getting. I was lucky I had my camera and snapped a quick picture.

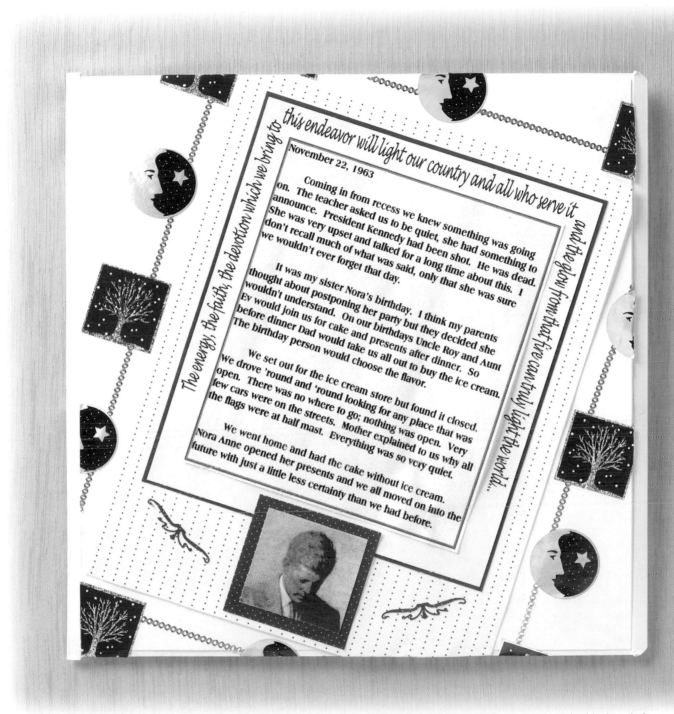

this endeavor will light our country and all who serve it and the glow from that fire can truly light the world...

The energy, the faith, the devotion which we bring to

November 22, 1963

Coming in from recess we knew something was going on. The teacher asked us to be quiet, she had something to announce. President Kennedy had been shot. He was dead. She was very upset and talked for a long time about this. I don't recall much of what was said, only that she was sure we wouldn't ever forget that day.

It was my sister Nora's birthday. I think my parents thought about postponing her party but they decided she wouldn't understand. On our birthdays Uncle Roy and Aunt Ev would join us for cake and presents after dinner. So before dinner Dad would take us all out to buy the ice cream. The birthday person would choose the flavor.

We set out for the ice cream store but found it closed. We drove 'round and 'round looking for any place that was open. There was no where to go; nothing was open. Very few cars were on the streets. Mother explained to us why all the flags were at half mast. Everything was so very quiet.

We went home and had the cake without ice cream. Nora Anne opened her presents and we all moved on into the future with just a little less certainty than we had before.

One swift moment in 1963 will remain etched in America's consciousness. Those who lived through it will always remember where they were when President John F. Kennedy was shot. Pennie Stutzman of Broomfield, Colorado, captured in words her feelings from a day unlike any other.

Cathleen Carew soon-to-be-Woodington and father John Joseph "Jack" Carew

During rehearsal, Cathy had to keep reminding her dad to smile. One final reminder and up the aisle we go!(Oh - Cathy was ready early, but for unknown reasons the ceremony began approximately ten minutes late.) Cathy remembered seeing Rose Heredia and then almost starting to cry so she quickly looked away. Tim was supposed to meet Cathy and her dad at the top of the aisle, however he said later that he was so busy thinking how beautiful Cathy looked that he stood rooted in his spot. Only after Cathy and Dad reached the top of the aisle and stood there, did Tim snap out of it and go get Cathy. We were really glad the ceremony was video tapped, especially since Cathy didn't remember hearing any of the trumpet music. The light through the stained glass hit the sequins on Cathy's dress and made her sparkle up on the altar.

Here we go up the aisle!

The planning is finished, the bride is blushing, and the church is packed with well-wishers. A wedding day goes by in a blur, but certain moments may stand out in your mind. Record them as did Cathy Woodington of Glendora, California.

An expectant parent harbors a hundred dreams and wishes for the family's newest addition. Dale Caliaro of Oviedo, Florida, made note of her myriad feelings and the love she felt before she ever held or beheld her child.

Expectation...

We found out that we would be blessed with a second child on Thanksgiving day! Well that's definitely something to be thankful for...

A new chapter in our lives is about to begin. We are both a little afraid... both excited...both wondering about the changes a new life will bring to our family...

Bethany is thrilled to find out there will be a little brother or sister joining her... She's telling everyone she is going to have a baby. She says there is a baby in her tummy too!

Nine months suddenly seems like such a short time to prepare... There is so much that needs to be done, and yet nine months seems almost an eternity to wait... What does this new baby look like? What kind of child will it be? The heart is already beating inside me, I am in awe of the precious gift that is growing inside my body...

Wonderment, Joy...

Gardening with Grandma

She would spend hours in the garden tending to her plants, watering, weeding, and cutting flowers for bouquets. This was a way of life for her.

Remembering Grandma Mildred Ann Ross (or Millie as everyone called her) brings back memories of her beautiful flower garden. She would spend hours in the garden tending to her plants, watering, weeding, and cutting flowers for bouquets. This was a way of life for her. She grew up on a farm and was surrounded by lush green corn fields and the family garden. When she married Grandpa Joe and they moved to the city, she brought a little bit of the country with her and had a garden of her own. Whenever I went to visit them, if it was nice outside, we would be in her garden. She would fix us lunch and we would set out on the patio. She would tell us stories about growing up on the farm. I felt so special that Grandma would spend the time to talk to me about her childhood and teach me about gardening. Now I have my own garden, and whenever I spend time out there, I remember that special feeling I had spending time with Grandma Millie.

To honor the memory of a departed loved one, Erikia Ghumm of Brighton, Colorado, journaled about her emotional bond with her Grandmother. Your writings may be the only way for future generations to connect with a wonderful human being.

Incorporating Other Voices

As you develop more confidence in your writing, you will also develop a "voice" that is uniquely your own. The voice will reflect the way you speak, your sense of humor and the way you view the world. It may, for example, be gentle and introspective or outspoken and glib. Once you're comfortable with your voice, you can start adapting it to accomplish many different kinds of writing tasks. The easiest way to modify your voice is to change the point of view in which you're writing. Writers refer to these as first person (I like to journal in my scrapbooks) and third person (Sara likes to write in her scrapbooks). This book, by the way, is written mostly in second person (You like to journal in your scrapbooks). First and second person lend a more casual sound to text, while third person is more neutral and formal. Most American newspapers are written in third person. Like a journalist, you can write about the thoughts and feelings of other people yet still keep your own voice. Try capturing real dialogue, in all of its imperfect splendor. Recording what other people think and say widens the scope of your writing, revealing much about not just you, but the world around you.

Pamela James of Ventura, California, captured the essence of the grandfather she'd never met by incorporating the first-person writing on the back of the photo and third-person thoughts provided by her father and grandmother.

Interviewing tips

A great interview is like a journey with a friend. You start in one place and travel to another together, with a lot of adventures in between. Here are some tips for great scrapbooking interviews:

1. Prepare your subject for the interview by letting her know what subjects you'd like to discuss.

2. Try tape-recording if that is comfortable for the subject. But take notes of important details such as names, dates, key words and special phrases just in case your recorder fails.

3. Come prepared with questions, but don't be afraid to deviate from your list.

4. Ask questions that you would want to be asked.

5. Ask open-ended questions instead of yes-or-no questions. Ask, "Why did you like your teacher?" not "Did you like your teacher?"

6. Don't pepper your subject with questions. Allow pauses to let your subject's answers soak in. If you give her a moment of silence, she may remember another relevant detail.

7. Listen attentively. Nod and make eye contact. Don't be so anxious to get to your next question that you don't listen to the answer your subject is giving.

8. Reflect back what you are hearing—"Is this what you said?"

9. Make sure you have the correct spelling of names.

10. If you're going to use direct quotes in your journaling, repeat them back to your subject for accuracy.

11. Conclude with a phrase such as, "What would you like to add?" or "What haven't I asked that I should have?" Let your subject know how she can get in touch with you if she thinks of anything later.

12. Always thank your subject.

Tools to Help You Journal

Your writing will evolve and improve as you practice, but there are also resources available to help you move along the learning curve more quickly. Reference books, a computer and some basic scrapbooking tools will ensure that your message is clear, concise and easy to read.

In the scrapbook page above, created by Julie Labuszewski, Littleton, Colorado, a journaling template was used to give the text a dynamic and fun look.

Journaling templates and rulers

Journaling templates provide countless shapes to guide your journaling. Simply pencil in the guidelines. After inking in your words, gently erase the pencil lines and nobody's the wiser. Some templates frame your words within cutout spaces; no lines needed. With placement grids, use a light box to project the grid's lines through your paper. Follow the lines, and you've got it made.

Computer

A computer is a powerful research, writing and design tool for those comfortable using it. The Internet makes searching for information easy. Online dictionaries, thesauri and quotation Web sites are free and accessible. A computer makes correcting, revising and retaining copies of your journaling quick. Word-processing programs liberate you by offering thousands of options for fonts, many type sizes, wide and narrow spacing and more. Most spell-checking features can catch errors, but they won't catch correctly spelled words that are used incorrectly (such as mixing "which" and "witch"). Photo-quality printers are becoming more affordable, but check with your printer manufacturer about archival inks.

Writing guide, dictionary and thesaurus

What to write and how to write it are the missions of many excellent writing guides available these days. For content, consider the books available about writing biographies and writing journals or diaries. For more about grammar, sentence structure and word usage, check out style guides such as *The Careful Writer: A Modern Guide to English Usage* by Theodore Menline Bernstein and *The Elements of Style* by William Strunk, Jr.

Before setting down your words in your scrapbook, check the dictionary to eliminate misspellings and verify definitions. Consult a thesaurus to find alternatives for overused words. Thesaurus formats vary, so become familiar with one before investing in a copy. An excellent alternative is *The Synonym Finder* by J.I. Rodale.

Stickers and preprinted journaling blocks

If you're just too scared to write directly on your pages, use journaling stickers or preprinted journaling blocks in a variety of designs. When your words are perfect, adhere the block to your page. Matching borders and accent stickers are available to tie your page together.

Making Design and Journaling Work Together

Words can be lovely to hear and just as beautiful to see. When they are considered a visual element of a scrapbook's page design, they become part of the art. The context of your page can guide you to the form your journaling should take. When telling a fun story, blur the line between words and art a little bit. For sensitive topics, you may want to "hide" your journaling in an envelope or pocket. If you have a lot to say, make a small book to include on your page. Soon you'll find that you look forward to coming up with new ways to display your journaling.

HOLD ON TO YOUR DIAPER

The first time mommy and daddy saw you roll over was quite an experience! You worked yourself from your back onto your stomach.

Apparently quite pleased with yourself, you looked around and giggled. Of course it wasn't long before you realized you were stuck!

SAMS ON A ROLL

To really make your journaling a visual part of your page, match the style of journaling to your page's theme. Tracy Haynes of Boynton Beach, Florida, mimicked her son's rolling by journaling along a rolling wavy line.

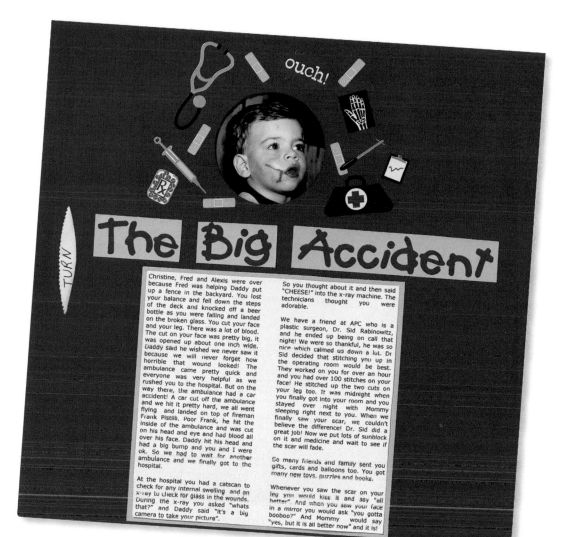

ouch!

The Big Accident

TURN

Christine, Fred and Alexis were over because Fred was helping Daddy put up a fence in the backyard. You lost your balance and fell down the steps of the deck and knocked off a beer bottle as you were falling and landed on the broken glass. You cut your face and your leg. There was a lot of blood. The cut on your face was pretty big, it was opened up about one inch wide. Daddy said he wished we never saw it because we will never forget how horrible that wound looked! The ambulance came pretty quick and everyone was very helpful as we rushed you to the hospital. But on the way there, the ambulance had a car accident! A car cut off the ambulance and we hit it pretty hard, we all went flying and landed on top of fireman Frank Pistilli. Poor Frank, he hit the inside of the ambulance and was cut on his head and eye and had blood all over his face. Daddy hit his head and had a big bump and you and I were ok. So we had to wait for another ambulance and we finally got to the hospital.

At the hospital you had a catscan to check for any internal swelling and an x-ray to check for glass in the wounds. During the x-ray you asked "whats that?" and Daddy said "it's a big camera to take your picture".

So you thought about it and then said "CHEESE!" into the x-ray machine. The technicians thought you were adorable.

We have a friend at APC who is a plastic surgeon, Dr. Sid Rabinowitz, and he ended up being on call that night! We were so thankful, he was so nice which calmed us down a lot. Dr Sid decided that stitching you up in the operating room would be best. They worked on you for over an hour and you had over 100 stitches on your face! He stitched up the two cuts on your leg too. It was midnight when you finally got into your room and you stayed over night with Mommy sleeping right next to you. When we finally saw your scar, we couldn't believe the difference! Dr. Sid did a great job! Now we put lots of sunblock on it and medicine and wait to see if the scar will fade.

So many friends and family sent you gifts, cards and balloons too. You got many new toys, puzzles and books.

Whenever you saw the scar on your leg you would kiss it and say "all better". And when you saw your face in a mirror you would ask "you gotta booboo?" And Mommy would say "yes, but it is all better now" and it is!

Some stories are simply too good to edit. If you need more space in which to journal, consider constructing a memory wheel. Chris Peters of Hasbrouck Heights, New Jersey, was able to incorporate five photos and lots of journaling into a single 12 x 12" page. For instructions see page 92.

...whenever you saw the scar on your leg you would kiss it and say, "all better."

If a square block of journaling would be awkward on your page, camouflage your journaling in a shape that flows with your design. Jeanne Ciolli of Dove Canyon, California, echoed the shape of her cropped photos with a journaling block that floats like a cloud.

Jazz up a long text block with doodles and bright colors. Melanie Mitchell of Overland Park, Kansas, gave extra punch to certain words with varying pen colors and weights. By breaking up lines of text with brighter visuals, you can pull your reader through the story to the end.

She loves to be wrapped up in towels after her shower, the more towels the better... she says they make her feel like a princess.

A flap or fold-out enables you to add journaling and extra photos. Liz Connolly of Sturbridge, Massachusetts, matched her fold-out to her theme by creating a fluffy towel out of fuzzy paper.

Your text doesn't always have to be black and white. Spice up your journaling with a splash of color. Emily Tucker of Matthews, North Carolina, made her journaling play off her title and color choices by matting certain words on coordinating colored papers.

Capture the story behind your photos... literally! If you're particularly inspired by a photo, let your journaling leap from a block to your photo mat. Holle Wiktorek of Fayetteville, North Carolina, bulleted descriptions and feelings on a photo mat to highlight important aspects of her relationship with her husband and family.

This is confusing...
Its not like they said
it was going to be...
We've never had
to be anywhere 5
days a week ever!

When journaling about certain events in life, you may feel like you're writing a book. Well, go ahead! Susan Badgett of North Hills, California, made her own spiral-bound, mini journaling album to record her thoughts and feelings on the day her son started kindergarten.

The content of your words tell a story, but sometimes the form they take can add extra detail. Experiment with turning your words into a meaningful part of your design. When Jadelyn Alvarez of Folsom, California, visited her husband's office with her son, she journaled the story on an office sticky note.

Characteristics of the Job or Task
Face-to-face interaction with customers (with the
exception of sales positions) required on a daily basis, and
the job task has phases of work in which the employee
spends most of the time working by him/herself.

Because of your design or the subject matter, you may not always want your journaling to be immediately apparent to the casual viewer. Simply slip a small sheet of journaling behind the top edge of a photo mat. Alex Bishop of Honolulu, Hawaii, utilized several pull-outs in order to tell the complete story of her daughter's hair adventures.

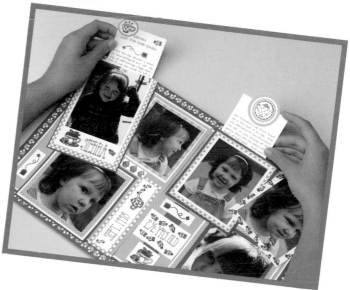

One day we were shopping at the grocery store and she picked out a bunch of hair bands. "Look mom, I look like a princess!" Hurray!

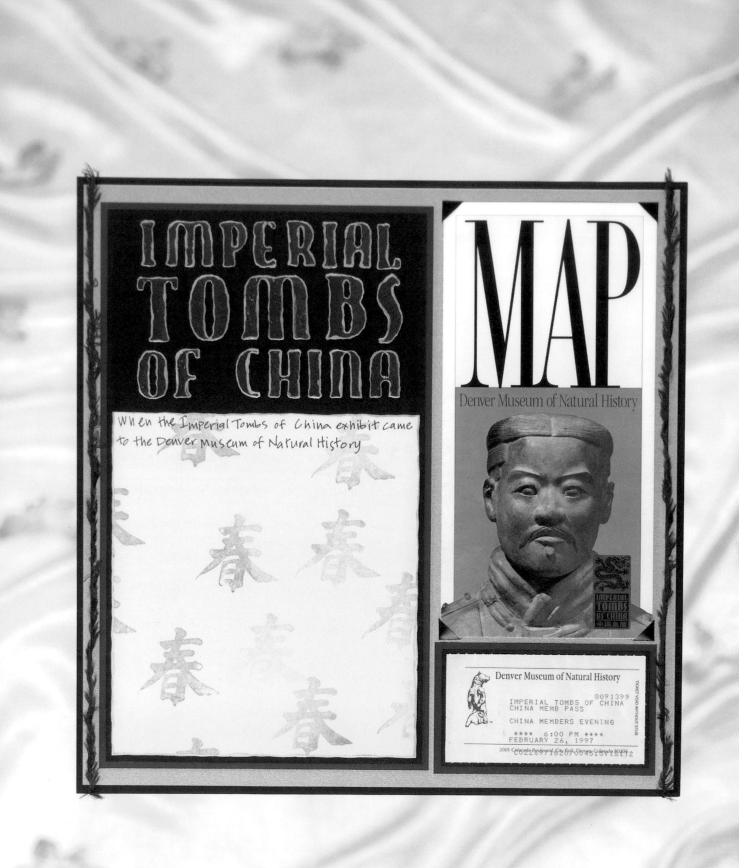

IMPERIAL TOMBS OF CHINA

MAP
Denver Museum of Natural History

WHen the Imperial Tombs of China exhibit came to the Denver Museum of Natural History

Denver Museum of Natural History

8091399
IMPERIAL TOMBS OF CHINA
CHINA MEMB PASS

CHINA MEMBERS EVENING

**** 6:00 PM ****
FEBRUARY 26, 1997

When Journaling Is Difficult

Even the most accomplished writers experience problems from time to time. Writing is very personal, and putting yourself on paper for all the world to see isn't easy. If you're facing writer's block or some other challenges, take comfort in knowing that you're in good company. The first step in staring down a writing issue is to classify the problem. Is it a technical hitch such as retro-fitting journaling onto a finished page? Or is it a creative issue, such as "writing around" missing photos? Perhaps you're unable to find the words needed to write about a particularly emotional topic. Take heart and then take a few moments to discuss the problem with your writer friends. They may have suggestions for over-coming your obstacles or recommendations of writing guides to consult. Pretty soon, you'll have a storehouse of successes to tap.

Overcoming Writer's Block

You're a writer now. So why are your hands cold and your palms sweaty when you grip your pen or touch your keyboard? Why does it seem as though your creative faucet has been turned off? It's called writer's block. The bad news is that it can hit any writer at any time. The good news is that there are ways to get the creative juices and words flowing once again.

1 If you're intimidated by writing, explore why. Be a detective, scouring your memory for people who implied that writing was difficult or your writing wasn't good enough. Was it your third-grade teacher? A supervisor at work? Don't be a victim. Get even by writing.

2 When preparing to journal, create a list of potential topics. Brainstorm by yourself or with a friend. Don't edit yourself. There's time for that later.

3 Poring over photos often helps break your writer's block. Try spinning a story to connect what otherwise appear to be unrelated photos.

4 Remember the basics: Ask who, what, when, where, why and how. Once you address those questions and write down the answers, you will often find that your writing wheels are in gear.

A group of unrelated photos can stump even the most avid journaler, but Angie Basden-Kauffman of West Lafayette, Indiana, invented an action-packed storyline to turn her tot into an international spy.

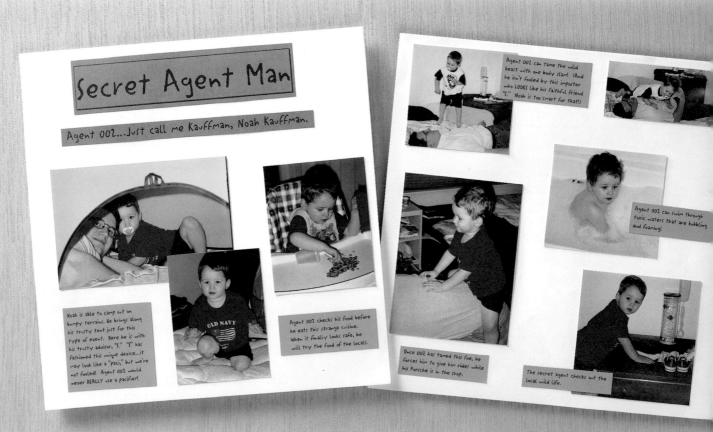

How We Met

Liesl   Mike

The Occasion: a singles Bible study
Where: Washington Crossing United Methodist Church
When: Friday, December 6, 1991
Who we were with: Nancy Glatfelter, Elyse Stirneman, Chuck Raphael.
How did we first bump into each other? I came out of the gym to get my purse, and I saw him on a bench.

If narrative journaling isn't flowing or doesn't feel right for your page, let it go. Focus instead on clearly recording the most important details about your photos. Liesl Walsh of Perkasie, Pennsylvania, documented the vital facts of a happy meeting by asking the basic questions—who, what, when, where and how.

5 Answer questions such as "How does this photo or memory make me feel? What smells, tastes, sounds and sights do I wish to record?"

6 Turn your ideas into an outline, planning how each idea will transition naturally into the next.

7 If a big blank page or screen intimidates you, try writing your initial ideas on sticky notes or scraps of paper. Or carry a cute little notebook to jot down ideas.

8 Some writers evolve a little icebreaker sentence or phrase to start every bit of writing— "The quick brown fox jumped over a lazy dog." Even if it's nonsense, you've written something and you're not facing that blank paper anymore.

9 Take a walk and think about it. Be sure to tuck your notebook into your back pocket for quick access.

10 Dress to write: Slippers, jeans and hair up in a ponytail may be your comfort zone. Or you may get motivated by dressing in business attire. Find what works.

11 Talk to a spouse, friend, child or dog about your message. Whatever you would reasonably tell them about your topic is probably worth writing down.

12 If no one's available to talk to about your topic, start writing about it in the form of a letter to a friend.

13 Write as you speak; this is what writers call finding your voice. Keep it simple.

14 Make a home for your writing; all you need is a desk, a nook or cranny where you enjoy being. Equip it with tools of the trade: pens and pencils, paper and a dictionary.

15 Join up with a writing buddy or a writing group. Get your whole crop group involved. An obligation to share your work gives you motivation to finish.

16 Set the mood for writing. Play music or light candles and incense. Do whatever it takes to put you in the right mindset.

17 Muse about what you wish to write as you lie in bed at night. Often you will find the piece has started to write itself in your mind when you wake up the next morning.

Mommies Loves

What can I say, I have the best & cutest kids around. I am so fortunate to be in a wonderful marriage and have two great kids & one more baby on the way. Yup, that is right I am 7 and a half months pregnant here. I am having another boy & can not wait to have that baby in my arms too. I believe♥, children are the seeds to happiness. We have planted our seeds & I ♥ can not wait to see what kind of blooming my children do as they grow up & mature. My life now somehow seems to be complete. My little bug-a-boo's are the most precious gifts I could ever get. They bring me such joy & happiness. I love being a mom & I love my life & most of all I love my family. 12/19/99

When you're having trouble describing the events captured in a photo, try another direction. Write about how the photo makes you feel. Seeing a portrait of herself with her two sons prompted Michele Rank of Cerritos, California, to write this touching and loving tribute to her family.

*I believe children are
the seeds to happiness.
We have planted our seeds
& I can not wait to see what
kind of blooming my children do
as they grow up and mature.*

Writing About the Hard Times

Living through painful or difficult experiences is hard enough. The last thing you may want to do is write about them. Yet writing is just what the doctor ordered. The very act of sitting down to record facts and feelings provides you with an outlet to release them. You move through your pain and, in a sense, leave some of it behind on your pages. Writing about the tough times is a therapeutic life habit to develop. It helps you look back and remember the details and lessons you learned, perhaps with sadness yet hopefully with understanding and peace.

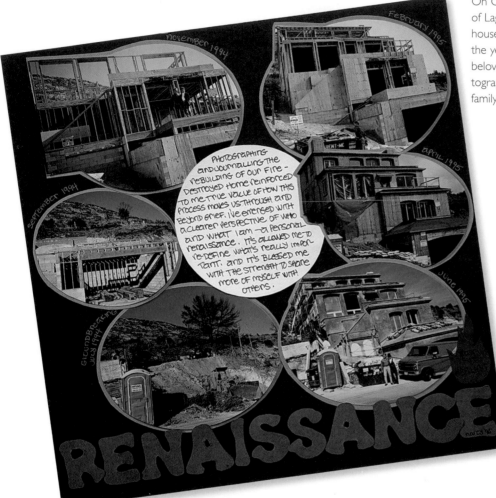

On October 27, 1993, Nancy Wagner of Laguna Hills, California, watched her house explode in flames. Lost were the years of remodeling work, two beloved cats, five generations of photographs and countless other precious family heirlooms.

Five generations of family keepsakes and precious memorabilia were destroyed and irreplaceable, but my journaling brought alive the memories of the past, the importance of the present, and the hope for the future.

When I saw the positive line my heart stopped and I gasped out loud in shock! After a few moments of letting it sink in I grinned so big and began to laugh as the joy just spilled out!

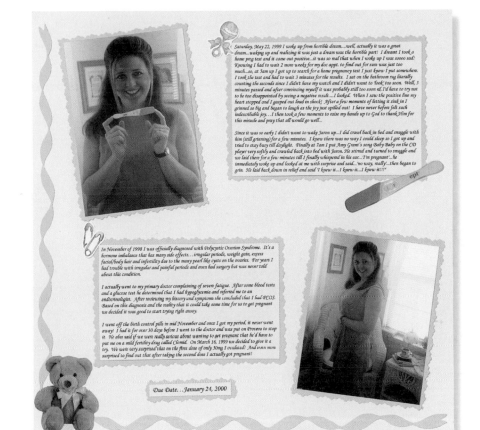

Saturday, May 22, 1999 I woke up from horrible dream...well, actually it was a great dream...waking up and realizing it was just a dream was the horrible part! I dreamt I took a home preg test and it came out positive...it was so real that when I woke up I was soooo sad! Knowing I had to wait 2 more weeks for my doc appt. to find out for sure was just too much...so, at 5am I got up to search for a home pregnancy test I just knew I put somewhere. I took the test and had to wait 3 minutes for the results. I sat on the bathroom rug literally counting the seconds since I didn't have my watch and I didn't want to look too soon. Well, 3 minutes passed and after convincing myself it was probably still too soon ol, I'd have to try not to be too disappointed by seeing a negative result...I looked. When I saw the positive line my heart stopped and I gasped out loud in shock! After a few moments of letting it sink in I grinned so big and began to laugh as the joy just spilled out! I have never before felt such indescribable joy...I then took a few moments to raise my hands up to God to thank Him for this miracle and pray that all would go well...

Since it was so early I didn't want to wake Jaron up...I did crawl back in bed and snuggle with him (still grinning) for a few minutes. I knew there was no way I could sleep so I got up and tried to stay busy till daylight. Finally at 7am I put Amy Grant's song Baby Baby on the CD player very softly and crawled back into bed with Jaron. He stirred and turned to snuggle and we laid there for a few minutes till I finally whispered in his ear...'I'm pregnant'...he immediately woke up and looked at me with surprise and said...'no way, really'...then began to grin. He laid back down in relief and said 'I knew it...I knew it...I knew it!!!'

In November of 1998 I was officially diagnosed with Polycystic Ovarian Syndrome. It's a hormone imbalance that has many side effects...irregular periods, weight gain, excess facial/body hair and infertility due to the many pearl like cysts on the ovaries. For years I had trouble with irregular and painful periods and even had surgery but was never told about this condition.

I actually went to my primary doctor complaining of severe fatigue. After some blood tests and a glucose test he determined that I had hypoglycemia and referred me to an endocrinologist. After reviewing my history and symptoms she concluded that I had PCOS. Based on this diagnosis and the reality that it could take some time for us to get pregnant we decided it was good to start trying right away.

I went off the birth control pills in mid November and once I got my period, it never went away! I had it for over 30 days before I went to the doctor and was put on Provera to stop it. He also said if we were really serious about wanting to get pregnant that he'd have to put me on a mild fertility drug called Clomid. On March 16, 1999 we decided to give it a try. We were very surprised that on the first dose of only 50mg I ovulated! And even more surprised to find out that after taking the second dose I actually got pregnant!

Due Date...January 24, 2000

God Will Take Care of You

May your troubled heart find peace and comfort in the knowledge that you are never alone.
May God's presence ease your trembling spirit and give you rest.
He knows how you feel.
He is well aware of your circumstances and ready to be your strength, your grace, and your peace.
He is close to cast sunlight into all of your darkened shadows, to send encouragement through the love of friends and family, and to replace your weakness with new hope.

God is your stronghold, and with Him as your guide, you need never be afraid.
No circumstance can block His love.
No grief is too hard for Him to bear.
No task is too difficult for Him to complete.
When what you are feeling is simply too deep for words and nothing anyone does or says can provide you with the relief you need,
God understands.
He is your provider today, tomorrow, and always.
And He loves you.
Cast all of your cares on Him... and believe.
– Linda E. Knight

The very day after I feeling out I was pregnant, I started to bleed. It really scared me and from that moment took away all my joy of being pregnant. My doc assured me bleeding can be normal. A few days later I started to have pain so Jaron took me to the UK. They weren't able to find much of anything wrong. They said I was either miscarrying or that everything is ok and the bleeding could be very normal in some pregnancies. I called my doctor a couple more times worried that something was wrong and he told me I was being paranoid and that it was normal pains of pregnancy.

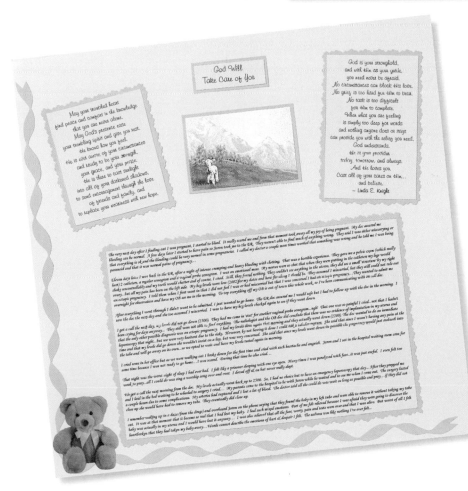

After struggling with infertility, Michelle Brownell of Lake Mary, Florida, finally conceived, only to suffer a heartbreaking loss. A few months later, she picked up a roll of film and found the joyful photos of the day she discovered she was pregnant. To honor her unborn child, Michelle decided to scrapbook the experience. "Our scrapbooks touch so much more than just our memories," she says. "They can be used as a tool to help bring comfort and heal the heart."

The day after her wedding, Caroline Lebel of Toronto, Ontario, Canada, lost her young brother to a sudden and devastating illness. She created this page so her daughter would remember the adventurous uncle who loved her dearly. "I felt the absolute necessity of getting down on paper even a portion of those little things that were "so Pierre" to me, that my daughter Serena know him even a little," Caroline says. "Writing the words down in her baby book had a permanence to it—even though she was only 11 months old when he passed away, she could now turn back to these pages later in life and smile a bit about this uncle she never really knew...maybe even see herself in him too."

We had last seen him dancing and having fun at the wedding, and he became very ill the next day.... It is so important to us that we never forget how special he was, and the great love he had for you.

When her father was only 57 years old, MaryJo Regier of Littleton, Colorado, watched as his health deteriorated and he slowly faded away. "It took me eight years to scrapbook the only photo I have of my dad during his illness," MaryJo says. "I just wanted to remember him as he was in all the years of photos I have—happy, healthy and alive. It was therapeutic though. I'm sure that if I had waited another eight years, so much of the emotion and detail would have faded with time and been lost."

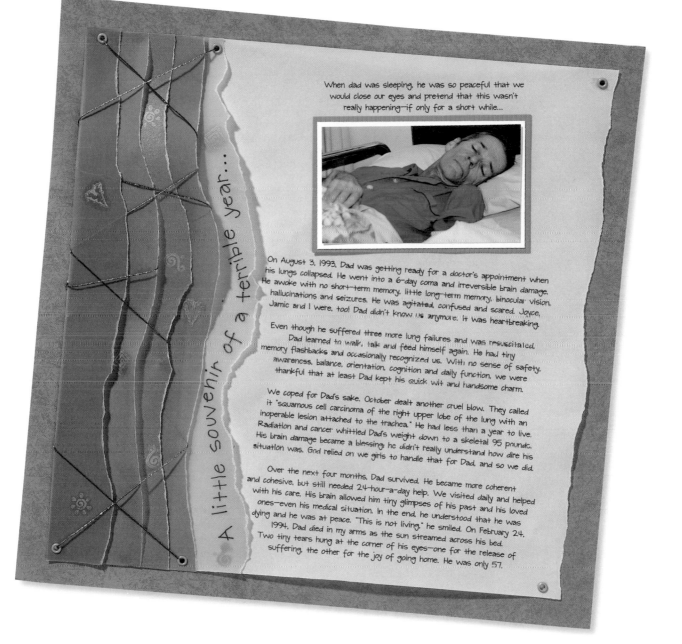

When dad was sleeping, he was so peaceful that we would close our eyes and pretend that this wasn't really happening—if only for a short while...

A little souvenir of a terrible year...

On August 3, 1993, Dad was getting ready for a doctor's appointment when his lungs collapsed. He went into a 6-day coma and irreversible brain damage. He awoke with no short-term memory, little long-term memory, binocular vision, hallucinations and seizures. He was agitated, confused and scared. Joyce, Jamie and I were, too! Dad didn't know us anymore. It was heartbreaking.

Even though he suffered three more lung failures and was resuscitated, Dad learned to walk, talk and feed himself again. He had tiny memory flashbacks and occasionally recognized us. With no sense of safety, awareness, balance, orientation, cognition and daily function, we were thankful that at least Dad kept his quick wit and handsome charm.

We coped for Dad's sake. October dealt another cruel blow. They called it "squamous cell carcinoma of the right upper lobe of the lung with an inoperable lesion attached to the trachea." He had less than a year to live. Radiation and cancer whittled Dad's weight down to a skeletal 95 pounds. His brain damage became a blessing; he didn't really understand how dire his situation was. God relied on we girls to handle that for Dad, and so we did.

Over the next four months, Dad survived. He became more coherent and cohesive, but still needed 24-hour-a-day help. We visited daily and helped with his care. His brain allowed him tiny glimpses of his past and his loved ones—even his medical situation. In the end, he understood that he was dying and he was at peace. "This is not living," he smiled. On February 24, 1994, Dad died in my arms as the sun streamed across his bed. Two tiny tears hung at the corner of his eyes—one for the release of suffering, the other for the joy of going home. He was only 57.

Two tiny tears hung at the corner of his eyes— one for the release of suffering, the other for the joy of going home.

Journaling About the Photos You Don't Have

When photos are missing in action or too few photos were taken to support a page theme, you may feel thrown for a loop. How can you replace missing photos with words? Think of it as the pop quiz you've been preparing for since opening this book. You now get to prove how far you've come by filling in the voids on your scrapbook page with words. Remember that descriptive and active words are vital to creating vibrant text. Describe not only people but settings. Capture snatches of dialogue to invest your journaling with texture and flavor. If you get stuck, shut your eyes and review mental snapshots—those photos you wished you were holding in your hand. Make note of your thoughts and feelings. When you open your eyes, transfer those insights to paper. If your page still cries out for artistic support, use memorabilia such as certificates, programs, ribbons and news clippings. Or create original artwork to display on the spreads.

Cameras are just machines, and as you know, machines have a nasty tendency to break down just when you need them most. Or you'll find yourself empty-handed at a special event you desperately want to record. Don't despair if you find yourself cameraless. Concentrate on creative ways to compensate. Like Dianne Kearns of Star Prairie, Wisconsin, you can fill a page and seize a memory with journaling and a paper-pieced visual accent.

No Pictures of Thanksgiving

Kelly forgot her camera at home, mine was in my car which I'd left at Steve's when I traded him for his truck, and Pat had the wrong film for her Polaroid. So fill in the images as you wish. Picture a fun day.

John and Annyce usually host Thanksgiving, but they went to her family's this year. Dad offered his house as long as he didn't have to do the cooking. So, on top of formally moving into my new house, I prepared a full turkey dinner for John Luger, Pat Luger, Kelly, Jesse and Cameron Ly, Kelly's friend, Dave Dudek, Matt Oswald and Steve and Trish Oswald. And me, Dianne Kearns.

When I got back from getting Steve's truck, Kelly and the boys were already there. She Said the boys were anxiously awaiting my return because they wanted to see the turkey.

As I took Jesse and Cameron downstairs to peer into the oven, Jesse asked, "How did you get the turkey? Did you shoot it?" With that question I knew they'd heard one too many Pilgrim stories and were expecting to see a turkey complete with feathers.

For whatever reason, I did not give them a straight answer, but decided to play with their heads. I replied, "No, you know Grammie doesn't approve of guns. So what I did was to run fast. Really fast. Faster than I'd ever run in my whole live. I ran and I ran. When I got close to the turkey, I made a giant leap through the air, grabbed the turkey and wrestled it to the ground."

Later Kelly said to me, "Whatever are you telling my kids? Jesse informed me that you told him you got the turkey by catching it and squishing it."

But aren't Grammies supposed to tell stories?

...Jesse asked, "How did you get the turkey? Did you shoot it?" With that question I knew they'd heard one too many Pilgrim stories...

It's a disappointment every scrapbooker must face—that awful sign that reads "No flash photography" or "No cameras allowed." Suddenly that Broadway play, concert or museum exhibit you've been waiting months to see is slipping by with nary a photograph. Before you leave that theater or exhibit hall, grab all the memorabilia you can find. Kimberly Edwards of Jacksonville, Florida, grabbed programs and playbills from her viewing of *The Phantom of the Opera.* Journaling, stickers and creative paper cutting formed a dynamic visual page and saved a precious memory.

Some experiences just can't be photographed. When Jami McCormick of Louisville, Colorado, went to scrapbook her son's first nightmare, her imagination and a cut-up museum brochure came together to illustrate something Jami herself had never seen. Her words tell the story of her son's reaction and Jami's own theory about what spurred the nightmare.

Adding Journaling to Finished Pages

It's never too late to add journaling to pages you created before you became a journalist. Often the simplest solution for retrofitting pages is the best. Page margins and edges of photos are great places to slip in a few words. Use a craft knife to cut a pocket in a mat in which to place newly journaled pages. Write on the die cuts you used. You may wish to augment the journaling on older spreads with pockets or page extenders. After all, scrapbooking is like life. You're always looking back through the lenses you have on today, seeing your experiences differently.

Add journaling by numbering your photos and then creating a reference list. Yuko Neal of Huntington Beach, California, was able to fit two reference lists into the blank space on her travel page. If your list won't fit on the page itself, attach it to a separate page.

If you can't find space to write or a way to make a pocket, create a vellum overlay like Stacey Shigaya of Denver, Colorado. Simply trace the rough outlines of your page and individual photos onto the vellum and add journaling in the open spaces. Slide the overlay into a page protector and place it right before the traced page in your album.

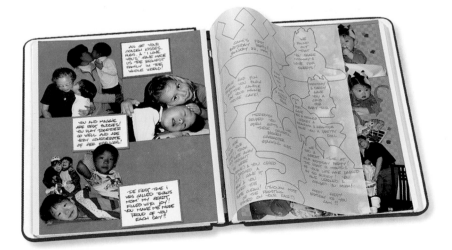

To accommodate the journaling for a wedding spread, Yuko Neal of Huntington Beach, California, attached a paper-cut wedding cake to the jeeping of two pages from her strap-hinge album. The back side of the wedding cake leaves room for additional photos.

Make your extra journaling look like you planned it all along by writing on separate pages or in a small notebook and then keeping it in a made-later pocket inside the front or back cover of your scrapbook. Nicole La Cour of Aurora, Colorado, found this to be the perfect technique when dealing with the small pages of an accordion album.

Improving Your Handwriting

Your penmanship doesn't have to be perfect for your journaling to be compelling. If it's readable and reflects your personality, it will add to your scrapbook pages. If your penmanship is illegible or you simply want to change its appearance, the first step toward improvement is to define the problem. Collect samples of your cursive handwriting and printing to examine. Consider everything from checks to recipes to love letters. Think of yourself as a handwriting doctor, trying to "diagnose" your ills. You're looking for letters that are unreadable or unattractive in some way. Are the letters uneven? Are they too far apart or too close together? Whatever ills plague your writing, you'll find help in the following tips. But remember, there is no "right" answer; your handwriting is a reflection of who you are. Someday, your descendants will find something that speaks to them in the way you crossed your "t's".

1 Collect others' handwriting you admire. Look through letters and postcards you have received. Determine what about the style you like and try to duplicate it.

2 Get a second opinion; show your handwriting to friends or relatives. Listen to their ideas on what you could do differently.

3 Set aside a few minutes each day to focus on improving your handwriting.

4 Purchase or make a pretty journal in which to practice. Pick something you will enjoy carrying and using often.

5 Find a pleasant, comfortable location with plenty of light in which to write.

6 Practice the alphabet one letter at a time. Make your "A" in both lower case and capitals. Write an entire line of "A's", joining them together as if they're one long word. Then write sentences that use words containing the letter "A". Try the same exercise with other letters.

7 Take note of how you hold your pen. Is it comfortable? Try different grips and different amounts of pressure to see what happens to readability.

8 Vary your slant, just for experimentation.

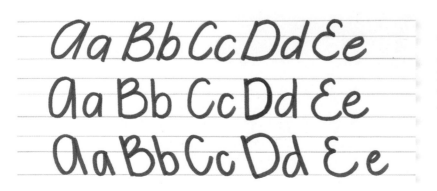

The slant of your letters imparts their appeal. Practice, practice, practice until your penmanship is pleasing to your eye. If you like what you see, chances are others will as well.

Fixing Journaling Mistakes

The key to fixing journaling goofs is making them look like they were part of your plan all along. Products like correction fluid cover imperfections seamlessly so you can try again. But fixing mistakes can simply be a job for your scrap bag. Find a coordinating color or pattern, write the corrected word or phrase on it, then adhere over the mistake. Stickers and die cuts also make great camouflage. They are available in hundreds of colors and themes. Choose one that supports your page concept and coordinates with its colors. Above all, apply the philosophy of Navajo rug weavers to your scrapbook: To be holy, each work must contain a small flaw.

A journaling "oops" can happen anywhere, but it doesn't need to destroy your scrapbook page. Use die cuts, stickers or punch art to artfully cover up mistakes, as on this page created by Erikia Ghumm of Brighton, Colorado. Photos Lydia Rueger, Arvada, Colorado

See the other side...

...of

Alaska

Forests of green and fields of blooming flowers aren't what you'd expect to see in Alaska, but take a **FAMOUS CRUISE** in the summertime, and you'll experience a wonderful world of contrasts. Mountain snowscapes and incredible icebergs loom overhead as you hike and kayak your way through the lush green landscapes of summer. So, load your camera and pack your bags for an incredible cruise to the other side.

Think Outside the Box: Other Styles

"The real voyage of discovery consists not in seeking new landscapes, but in having new eyes."

-Marcel Proust, novelist

Translating thoughts clearly from your mind to the page is the beginning of great writing. After clarity comes creativity. Now is the time to play, to experiment, to expand. Write your own travel brochure. Compose a poem. Crown yourself editor-in-chief of your own newspaper. Tell a story in pictures. Don't feel constrained to journal the same way on every page. As long as you are sharing your thoughts and feelings in words, there are no rules to govern the form your words take. A particular memory or photo may inspire you to try something new. Let it carry you to new journaling territory and break you free of the journaling box.

Bullet Journaling

There are no hard and fast rules about how your journaling should be structured. So forget all those old edicts that you must write in full sentences and must have tidy paragraphs. If all you want to do is record basic information, bullets are a perfect option. Bullet journaling is also a great choice for those times when you have more to say than space in which to say it.

Cathy Driedger of Calgary, Alberta, Canada, captures the highlights of her children's progress every six months. Bullets allow her to record priceless milestones while leaving room for adorable photos.

Dictionary Journaling

Define the qualities of a person or event through dictionary journaling. The well-known dictionary format provides an easy way to consolidate and structure your ideas. Look to other reference books for more creative journaling ideas. Why not create a thesaurus-style page to capture the synonyms that describe your spouse's personality? Or create an encyclopedia-type entry to describe your family vacation. Inspiration is as close as your local library's reference section.

Helen Rumph of Las Vegas, Nevada, summarized her son's tough attitude with three dictionary entries. Her journaling is easy to write and easy to read.

Recipe Journaling

Scrapbooks are a great place to preserve family recipes, but recipe-inspired journaling is more than just a cookbook of culinary favorites. Use recipe journaling to list the "ingredients" that make something, or somebody, special. With a teaspoon of imagination, a pinch of inspiration, some photos and a pen you can whip up an appetizing recipe page.

Michele Brynell of Fort Worth, Texas, wrote recipes for disaster to describe three of her son's messy misadventures. Recipe journaling provides a new way to relate your little one's food-related "accidents."

Timeline Journaling

Condensing twenty years of information into a paragraph is like trying to cram twenty years' worth of pictures onto one scrapbook spread. You'll find the job more doable with timeline journaling. A timeline is the perfect way to display a plethora of events on an organized, readable page.

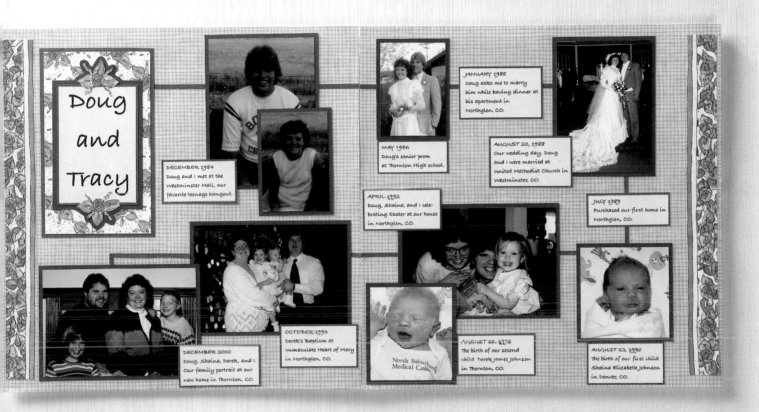

Tracy Johnson of Thornton, Colorado, was able to compress sixteen years of her relationship with her husband by creating a timeline. Page design by Erikia Ghumm of Brighton, Colorado

December 1984, Doug and I met at the Westminster Mall, our favorite teen hangout...January 1988, Doug asks me to marry him while having dinner at his apartment in Northglenn, CO...August 12, 1990, the birth of our first child, Shaina Elizabeth Johnson in Denver, CO.

Postcard Journaling

Having a wonderful time? Wish your scrapbook were there? Send yourself a postcard from the road detailing all the fun (or not-so-fun) events as they unfold. When you finally return home and are ready to scrapbook about your travels, your journaling will be in your mailbox waiting for you. With the journaling finished, you can concentrate on starting, and quickly completing, your travel pages.

Susan Smith of Suwanee, Georgia, sent herself this postcard while visiting the Greek island of Rodos. She attached the postcard itself to her page for instant journaling. The stamp and postmark serve as memorabilia of a unforgettable trip.

Classified Ad Journaling

Wanted: An innovative way to journal. If that's on your wish list, then classified ad journaling may be just what you're looking for. It's easy, no experience is necessary and the benefits are exceptional. Simply journal as though you are writing a classified ad. It's a great way to add humor to your album or just convey information in an original format.

Shona Ann Geier of Des Plaines, Illinois, wrote this want ad to list the characteristics needed for a mother of a baby and toddler. She captures the daunting challenges and the sweet rewards of motherhood with humor and feeling.

Acrostic Journaling

"What's in a name?" For scrapbookers, a name can be a jump-off point for journaling inspiration. Begin by writing down the name of a person about whom you wish to journal. Then write short phrases beginning with each letter within the name. The phrases should describe or relate to the named person. If you wish, a word can always be substituted for a name. Either way, you'll find it easier to write when you have those first letters down on paper.

Kori Steckley of Camas, Washington, used acrostic journaling to honor her husband alongside his graduation photo. She used his name as a starting point for a loving dedication.

Step-by-Step Journaling

Many instructional manuals are dry reading, but who wouldn't pore over a how-to pamphlet for putting together a memorable life experience? Step-by-step journaling breaks down the steps needed to carry out any activity you may want to record in your scrapbook. It's a great way to liven up your albums and acknowledge each element that contributes to making a memorable experience.

Pretend to admire the presents while actually deciding the one you want...Grab the present...If they are closing in on you, drop the present and run to safety.

Courtney Charoenpap of Pine Grove, Louisiana, recorded her daughter's steps for gift grabbing in a humorous holiday page. Page design by Pamela Frye of Denver, Colorado

Fairy Tale Journaling

Once upon a time there was a scrapbooker who wanted to add something special to her pages. Having misplaced her wand, she reached for her pens instead and transformed her writing into a charming story through fairy tale journaling. You too can add magic to your pages by adopting a storytelling voice. It will transform your text and assure that future generations will read it happily ever after.

Christi Flynn of Henderson, Nevada, found the perfect subject for fairy tale journaling—a Renaissance fair. Using a journaling style that complements your topic helps create a unified page.

Once upon a time there was a merry group of wenches and rogues who traveled the lands from near and far in search of feast, fine ale, magical mead and good company....

Poetic Journaling

To think that I should ever see a scrapbook page with poetry. You don't have to be Joyce Kilmer to tell a story in verse. Just let your creative juices and your ink flow. But if your muse simply isn't speaking up, check out poetry collections in books or on the Internet. You're sure to find something that expresses your feelings.

One Fine Day in May

One fine day in May
Karrah and Derek came out to play.
There were smiles galore
As they enjoyed the great outdoors!

Birds singing,
Beautiful shades of green everywhere,
Flowers blooming,
Their fragrance intoxicating the air.

It's time once again to celebrate
Our very wonderful fate—
Enjoying this beautiful spring day!
Come one, come all, it's time to play!

Joellyn Borke Johnston of Des Moines, Iowa, was inspired by fine weather and her children's playful mood to compose this joyful ode to spring.

Found Journaling

The written word is everywhere, from brochures and maps to programs and fliers. Take advantage of the wealth of these printed materials. Include them in your scrapbooks and you'll have instant journaling. Or use guidebooks, the Internet and other sources to gather information that can help you write well-informed, interesting text to accompany your photos.

Tree Cutting at
Genesee Mountain

How did this forest get here?
Forests have always played an important role in Colorado's history—from the time of the Native Americas, who used wood in rock homes and tepees; to the early towns that were sustained by harvested wood; to today when we depend on the forests for clean water, recreation, and wood for paper and lumber. Brian and I ar are Colorado Natives and love our beautiful mountains.

Why do we need to cut these trees?
Information from the Genesee Mountain Park says that cutting Christmas trees helps reduce the wildfire hazard and makes room for the remaining trees to grow. For us, cutting a tree for Christmas is tradition. Every year Brian, Becca and I go up to the mountains to cut our tree. We always bring our dogs and I make hot apple cider.

Which trees will I see here?
Park information says that the best species for Christmas trees found in the park are Douglas fir, Ponderosa pine, Lodgepole pine and Colorado blue spruce. We usually pick a tall Douglas fir or Lodgepole pine. The taller the tree, the stronger the branches are at the top.

For us, cutting a tree for Christmas is tradition... We always bring our dogs and I make hot apple cider.

Erikia Ghumm of Brighton, Colorado, gathered a map and fliers from the Genesee Mountain Park to beef up the journaling on her Christmas tree-cutting page.

Calendar Journaling

Do you do most of your writing on the family calendar? The notes you make on your calendar reveal important details about the activities in which you and your family are involved. That's where you record both the frequent happenings that fill your days as well as the once-a-year milestones and events. Include all that information in your scrapbooks as calendar journaling!

Adrienne Marko of Evergreen, Colorado, and her family had something happening every day during December 2000. A calendar page is an easy way to fit a lot of informative details on one page. Page design by Pamela Frye of Denver, Colorado

Newspaper Journaling

Newspaper journalists learn to pack a lot of information into a few short inches. You can do the same. Pick up your local daily for inspiration. Try your hand at writing your own "news" story featuring the most notable people and events in your life. For extra fun, include quotes from the story's major players.

"I have the wrong card" exclaims Trish. This says "Merry Christmas Aunt"...I'm not an aunt. WOW...I'm going to be an aunt!! All the while, Grandma Kensinger stands in disbelief!

Beth Gould of Midland, Texas, announced her pregnancy with telling Christmas cards. With the help of her friend Sarah Barrett, Beth documented the event in her scrapbook, adopting newspaper-style writing and newspaper-inspired design.

Perspective Journaling

If you're feeling generous, you may wish to consider including other people's journaling in your scrapbook. Just hand over pen and paper and ask them to write down their take on events showcased on your pages. You'll receive back a revealing handwriting sample and a fresh point of view. You may be surprised by what your contributing writers have to say and at how much their journaling adds to your spreads. Their perspectives can shine a different light and add a more well-rounded view of any event.

Kim Branson of Eagle River, Alaska, let her husband, Roger, write down his recollections of their engagement. Although they agreed upon the specifics of their shared experience, she and her husband each have a distinct way of detailing the event.

Top-Ten Journaling

List making is easy and so is top ten journaling. Both help you order and prioritize your thoughts. Think of top ten journaling as a grocery list. Your points don't have to be connected, and the order in which they appear doesn't matter as much as the content. Just scatter your journaling blocks about the page for fun and informative reading.

For a touching tribute to her mother, Stacey Shigaya of Denver, Colorado, gathered pictures depicting their life together. She then wrote thoughtful sentiments about why she loves her mother.

Correspondence Journaling

What would you say if you could speak directly to future generations? What truths would you share? What stories would you tell? Through your scrapbook you have the astounding opportunity to introduce yourself to those you may never meet. Write them a letter and post it in your scrapbook. Include letters written by others. And don't forget about other forms of correspondence—postcards, greeting cards and even e-mails are wonderful ways to chat with the future.

Meg,

You're 3 1/2 months old now. It seems sometimes like you've always been in our lives and sometimes like you're brand new. You can smile, laugh and razz. Right now you're lying on my lap sleeping. It must not be a good sleep because you keep making sad faces and sounds. Noah and I are stroking your head and telling you, "we're here, it's alright."

Your dad and I must have the same conversation every day: "you're such a wonderful baby! We can't believe you're so happy and sweet. She's so awesome! We're so lucky!"

Some days you sleep a lot, some days you are very active, some days you nurse a lot. Every day, though, we count you as another of our greatest blessings from God. We love you, Meg!

Tammy Griffith of Columbus, Georgia, keeps a notebook in which she writes thoughts about her children. When she scrapbooks, she uses the notes to flesh out her journaling and leave messages her children can read and enjoy when they are grown.

Rebus Journaling

Sometimes a picture's worth a thousand words, and sometimes it's worth just one. When rebus journaling, you use pictures in place of words. Just construct your phrase, leaving slots to insert images. You can rebus journal with photographs, stickers, stamps, punches, doodles, anything that can visually stand in for a word or idea.

Leah Socorro of Franklin, Massachusetts, illustrated a popular Christmas song with photos of her little ones. The rebus journaling conveys the festive feeling behind the lyrics. Page design by Pamela Frye of Denver, Colorado

Comic Strip Journaling

Didja hear the one about the scrapbooker who used comic strip journaling in her album? She captured her favorite jokes, funny stories, youthful hijinks and travel misadventures in a panel format. You can too. It's fun to do, and your audience will keep laughing, and reading, to the punch line. Sometimes the photos you have suggest a unique style of journaling.

When Rachel Smith of Vancouver, British Columbia, Canada, cropped out undesirable backgrounds from photos of her son, the silhouettes of his mischief made a perfect comic strip.

When Mommy's not looking I can write on doors and walls! ...I wonder where James is?...I'd better go find him...Hah! I found the baby bath soap! My hair is coated in soap—now what?...Oops, Mommy has caught me!!!

Other Styles of Journaling

Many scrapbookers are thinking off the tablet line and outside of the box when it comes to journaling. Often, all it takes to make the leap from conventional note-taking to creative storytelling is a bit of confidence and inspiration. This gallery of terrific scrapbooking pages should provide both.

Document the game of life on a scrapbook page. Keep track of milestones on a board that tracks your progress. This playful journaling style is sure to be a winner for all ages. Kathleen Fritz, St. Charles, Missouri

Slobber attack. After running or eating, wipe your mouth on your opponent's hair, skin, or nice clothes.

Create a Puppymon (Pokemon) card for your best four-legged friend. Or make a baseball card for the sports nut in your life. Record the vital stats that make your subject collection-worthy. Lucinda Price, Powell, Tennessee

Family newsletters, like newspapers, are making their way onto the Web. Keep a printout of your family's Web page in your scrapbook to document family events and twenty-first century technology. Rachel and Stuart Tomares, Rockville, Maryland

Daniel Tomares... the only three-year-old participating in the astronaut training program.

"Take Tommy to soccer, 3:00." "Take Susie to piano, 4:15." "Take puppy to vet, 5:00." All those penned reminder notes that keep track of your family's obligations also record your daily activities. Hold on to them and include them in your albums as journaling. Priscilla Simon, Atlanta, Georgia

Forget standing in line at the DMV. Although it may not be quite as official, you can hand out your own license to drive, have fun or work. A cute portrait completes any identification card. Mena Spodobalski, Reno, Nevada

Gather the evidence you need to solve a household crime, and then take it down for the record in a faux police report. Don't forget to include the final verdict for a fully documented case. Kristi Hazelrigg, Washington, Oklahoma

Has your little buckaroo gone over to the wrong side of the law? Or maybe your spouse needs to be brought to scrapbooking justice. Put out a warrant with a wanted poster. Cathryn Wooton, Richmond, Virginia

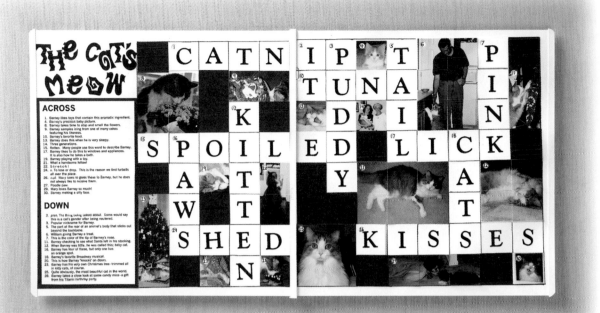

Creating your own crossword puzzle isn't as hard as it may look. Start with a list of words related to your subject, and then write down questions that will prompt readers to come up with the applicable word. Mary Burke, Franklin, Tennessee

Creating book jacket bios

As the family's historical documenter and designated camera-holder, your likeness may not show up often in your scrapbook. But it's easy to reveal a bit about yourself in a book jacket biography. Include your likes and dislikes, hopes and fears, what you enjoy about scrapbooking and any little insights you hope to share. You are a part of the history you're recording, and future generations will be as interested in you as those featured more often on your pages.

About the Author

Mary Ellen Jones enjoys all crafts, especially scrapbooking and water color painting. She loves going to basketball games and watching old movies. She is a self-proclaimed Disney fanatic and takes a vacation to either Disneyland or Disney World every other year.

Making a memory wheel *(as seen on page 45)*

1. Cut two 10½" circle "wheels." Glue together for strength. Trim outer edge with zigzag scissors for firm grip when turning wheel. Insert brad fastener through center of wheel and attach to center of background page. Spin wheel to ensure that it spins freely on page.

2. Photocopy photo pattern below; enlarge to 200 percent to fit a 12 x 12" scrapbook page. Cut five horizontal photos using pattern, positioning narrow part of the pattern at lower edge of photo subject. Mount photos securely on wheel with narrow bottoms surrounding center of wheel .

3. Use a circle cutter to cut a 2¾" window opening 1½" down at center of cover paper. Place window opening over wheel, centering one photo in the window. Lay window cover over mounted background and wheel; line up all edges. Use a small saucer to trace a curved 4" line to mark slot for wheel on window cover. Trace the line on paper over edge of wheel below and 1" from paper edge (Figure 3). Slot should point to left if wheel will turn on left side of page, right if wheel turns on right side of page. Remove window cover; cut open slot.

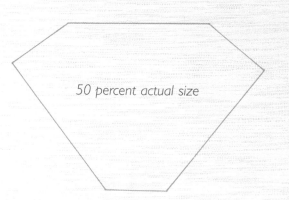

4. Place cover on background; slide edge of wheel through curved slot (Figure 4). Adhere cover to background at corners and edges, without capturing any of the wheel. Journal about the wheel's photos; decorate as desired.

50 percent actual size

Grammar Guide

If your grammar hasn't had a tuneup since grade school, check out this quick reference guide for troubleshooting the most commonly made mistakes. And remember, every rule has its exceptions, so consult a more detailed grammar book if you have further questions.

Comma Use
Always use a comma:
- to separate items in a list
- before "but," "and," and "or" if (and only if) the parts of the sentence before and after that word can be sentences on their own
- before and after phrases starting with "which" (don't use commas around phrases starting with "that")
- after "yes" and "no" at the beginning of sentences
- around someone's name if you're talking to him or her
- between adjectives describing the same thing

Possessive
- For singular words, use 's.
- For plural words, use s'.
- For names that end in s, either form is correct.

Plurals of letters and numbers
- For plurals of one letter, use "'s" (Ex. p's and q's).
- For plurals of numbers and more than one letter, just add "s" (Ex. 1980s and CDs)

Who vs. whom
Try this trick—if you can replace it with "he," use "who." If you can replace it with "him," use "whom."

Me vs. I
This usually only trips up people when someone else is added to the sentence. For example, "He took a picture of Tom and _____." Take out the other person, and it's obviously "me"—"He took a picture of me." Still use "me" when you add Tom back in—"He took a picture of Tom and me."

Possessive singular and plural pronouns
When nouns are plural, their possessive pronoun is "their." (Ex. Students should bring their books.) When nouns are singular, their possessive pronoun is "his," "her" or "its." (Ex. A student should bring his or her book.) It's awkward, but that's grammatically correct. (If you can, try to reword the sentence.)

The following words are always singular and should use "his or her."
- any word ending in "one" (anyone, no one, everyone, etc.)
- any word ending in "body" (anybody, nobody, everybody, etc.)
- each

Page contributors

Alvarez, Jadelyn, 50
Badgett, Susan, 49
Basden-Kauffman, Angie, 54
Bishop, Alexandra, 51
Borke Johnston, Joellyn, 79
Bowler, Kim, 16
Branson, Kim, 83
Brownell, Michelle, 59
Brynell, Michele, 72
Burke, Mary, 91
Caliaro, Dale, 38
Capener, Laurie, 24
Ciolli, Jeanne, 46
Connolly, Liz, 47
Driedger, Cathy, 70
Edwards, Kimberly, 63
Flynn, Christi, 78

Fritz, Kathleen, 88
Frye, Pamela, cover, 6, 19, 26, 68, 77, 81, 86
Gartland, Nicole, 11
Geier, Shona Ann, 75
Ghumm, Erikia, cover, 33, 39, 52, 67, 73, 80
Ginn, Brandi, 12, 34
Gould, Beth, 82
Griffith, Tammy, 85
Haynes, Tracy, 44
Hazelrigg, Kristi, 90
James, Pamela, 40
Kearns, Dianne, 62
Klassen, Pam, cover, 14, 15
Labuszewski, Julie, 42

La Cour, Nicole, 65
Lebel, Caroline, 60
Mayberry, Tami, 36
McCormick, Jami, 63
Mitchell, Melanie, 46
Neal, Yuko, 64, 65
Parrish, Sandi, 20, 21
Peters, Chris, 45
Pieper, Lori, 18
Price, Lucinda, 88
Rank, Michele, 8, 57
Regier, MaryJo, 61
Rumph, Helen, 71
Sharp, Michelle, 22
Shigaya, Stacey, 64, 84
Simon, Priscilla, 89

Smith, Rachel, 87
Smith, Susan, 74
Spodobalski, Mena, 90
Steckley, Kori, 76
Stutzman, Pennie, 37
Tansey, Deidre, 23
Tomares, Rachel and Stuart, 89
Torres, Yvonne, 10
Trachtman, Kimberly, 32
Trent, Lisa R., 25
Tucker, Emily, 48
Wagner, Nancy, 58
Walsh, Liesl, 55
Wiktorek, Holle, 48
Woodington, Cathy, 38
Wooton, Cathryn, 90

Credits

cover
Background paper: Provo Craft; blue patterned paper: Magenta; red patterned paper: A.W. Cute; cream patterned paper: Making Memories

page 6 School Nights at the Gerbrandts'
Border papers: Magenta, Scrap Ease; tan patterned paper: source unknown; sticker letters: Debbie Mumm; checkerboard: Debbie Mumm

page 8 A Gift For Max
Patterned paper and present stamp: Close To My Heart

page 10 The Two Shall Become One
Hand-drawn leaves and hearts on vine; red cardstock; decorative scissors: Fiskars

page 11 Grandma's Garden
Font: CK Journaling from the Creating Keepsakes Best of Creative Lettering CD; patterned paper (clouds): source unknown; lotus, teardrop and leaf punches: EK Success

page 12 Brinley Nicole Ginn
(Design Brandi Ginn, Lafayette, Colorado)
Vellum: DMD; embossed paper: NRN Designs; Dainty font: Lettering Delights by Inspire Graphics; flower eyelets: The Stamp Doctor

pages 14-15 Camping
Patterned papers: Provo Craft; square punch: Emagination; lettering stamps: Stampin' Up!

page 16 Grandpa Scott
Fish stickers: Mrs. Grossman's

page 18 Jana Lynn married James Gene
Template: Time And Again wedding from C-Thru Ruler; Vellum paper: source unknown

page 19 Friends
(Photos Dawn Mabe, Lakewood, Colorado; Design Pamela Frye, Denver, Colorado)
Leaf punch: Emagination; patterned paper: Scrappin' Dreams; sticker letters: SEI

pages 20-21 The Trip
Die-cut flowers and leaves: source unknown; lettering template: Cock-A-Doodle; font: CK Journaling from Creating Keepsakes

page 22 Special Touches/Glitches
Lucida Sans Unicode font: MS Word; wedding album pages: Creative Memories; Ripple scissors: Fiskars

page 23 Cayra of So Many Colours
Patterned paper: Hallmark; decorative scissors: Fiskars

page 24 When I Was a Teenager
Swirl and flower punches: Family Treasures; round flower and peace hands stickers: Stickopotamus; smile face stickers: source unknown

page 25 All About Me
Moon die cut: Ellison; shop stickers: Mrs. Grossman's

page 26 Our Family
(Photos Shawna Rendon, Thornton, Colorado; Design Pamela Frye, Denver, Colorado) Patterned paper: Making Memories; journaling template: C-Thru Ruler; tree die cuts: Deluxe Cuts

page 32 Mom Blew the Shofar Hard
Sticker letters: Creative Memories; music note die cuts: Creative Memories; ¼", ⅛" and ¹⁄₁₆" circle punches

page 34 Eckerts Farm
(Design Brandi Ginn, Lafayette, Colorado)
Patterned paper: Making Memories; vellum: DMD; font: Cock-A-Doodle; lettering template: watermelon lowercase by Scrap Pagerz

page 36 The Simple Things
Blue and white dots patterned paper: The Paper Patch; red plaid paper: Keeping Memories Alive; star punch: Marvy Uchida; font: VladimirScrD from Print Artist by Sierra

page 37 JFK
Moons and trees stickers: Mrs. Grossman's; silver band: Class A Peels by Mark Enterprises; patterned paper: Close To My Heart; crown border punch: McGill

page 38 Church of the Good Shepherd
Church die cut: Creative Memories; small heart and teardrop corner lace edge punches: Family Treasures; flower and butterfly stickers: Mrs. Grossman's

page 39 Gardening With Grandma
Patterned paper: Club Scrap

page 40 Oscar Lawrence Yokee
Wood veneer paper: Paper Adventures; patterned paper: source unknown; teardrop corner lace edge punch: Family Treasures; lotus punch: EK Success; ash leaf punch: Martha Stewart

page 44 Hold Onto Your Diaper
Diaper alphabet stickers: Stickopotamus; patterned paper: NRN Designs; wavy ruler: Creative Memories

page 45 The Big Accident
Doctor stickers: Frances Meyer; letter stickers: Provo Craft

page 46 Haleakala
Sun die cut: Ellison; sunset paper: Wübie Prints; font: Jeanne Personal from Lettering Delights by Inspire Graphics

page 47 Shannon's All Wrapped Up
Lettering template: log cabin from Frances Meyer; white fuzzy paper: Paper Adventures; Zig Writers pens: EK Success; blue cardstock; bleach; bubble stamp: source unknown

page 48 Hats
Chalks: Craf-T Products

page 48 Family Ties
Template: EK Success; Zig Writers black pen: EK Success; letter stickers: Stickopotamus; twine: source unknown; red, sand and dark brown cardstock: DMD Industries; font: CK Handprint from Creating Keepsakes Lettering Combo CD; Pop Dots™: All Night Media

page 49 Will Does Kindergarten
Patterned paper: Provo Craft; wood grain stamped paper: Coop Stamps; scissors: Provo Craft; stamps: All Night Media, Inkadinkado, Judikins, Posh Impressions, Rubber Stampede, Stampin' Up!, Stamps "N" Memories, Toomuchfun Rubberstamps; bus picture frame and stickers: Creative Imaginations; sticker letters: Provo Craft; die cuts: Westrim Crafts; punches: Family Treasures, McGill

page 50 Our Little Executive
Burlap patterned paper: Hot Off The Press; Post-It Notes: 3M; fonts: from MS Word

page 51 Sierra Sept. 1998
Rubber stamps: All Night Media; Zig Writers markers: EK Success; circle punch: Family Treasures; patterned paper: The Paper Patch

page 52 Imperial Tombs of China
(Design Erikia Ghumm, Brighton, Colorado) Stampabilities Asian stamp: Crafts, Etc.; 3-D Crystal Lacquer: Sakura; fibers: Adornments; photo corners: 3L

page 54 Secret Agent Man
Cardstock: Bazzill; font: Litterbox ICG from The Print Shop Premier Edition by Image Club Graphics

page 55 Liesl & Mike: How We Met
Hand-drawn hearts and leaves; heart sticker: R.A. Lang

page 57 Mommies Loves
Patterned paper: Close To My Heart; ink pad: Marvy Uchida; markers and rubber stamps: Close To My Heart; font: Grapevine from Creating Keepsakes

page 58 Renaissance
Decorative scissors: Fiskars

page 59 God Will Take Care of You
Stickers: Frances Meyer; decorative scissors: Fiskars; font: source unknown

page 60 Uncle Pierre Lebel
Green mulberry paper: PSX; patterned paper: Hot Off The Press; border stickers: Mrs. Grossman's

page 61 A Little Souvenir of a Terrible Year...
Vellum: Paper Adventures; font: Creating Keepsakes; rubber stamps: All Night Media; cord: Lion Brand Yarn Co.; eyelets: Impress Rubber Stamps

page 62 No Pictures of Thanksgiving
Turkey clip art: Coral Draw; decorative scissors: Fiskars; patterned paper: Keeping Memories Alive; sticker letters and beige paper: Paper Adventures

page 63 The Phantom of the Opera
Colored pencils: Prismacolor by Berol; stickers: Mrs. Grossman's

page 63 Travis' First Nightmare
Patterned paper: Masterpiece Studios; yellow cardstock; font: Chiller from MS Word; star die cut: Katee's Cut-Ups

page 64 Budapest
Lettering template: C-Thru Ruler; stickers: Creative Memories; patterned paper: Frances Meyer

page 65 Tom & Lynda's Wedding
Patterned paper: Frances Meyer; flower stickers: Mrs. Grossman's

page 67 St. Lucia
Die cut leaves: Deluxe Cuts; palm tree sticker: Creative Imaginations; vellum

butterfly: DMD Industries; photo frame: Amscan; die-cut flower and swirls: Cut-It-Up

page 68 See the Other Side of Alaska (Photos Michele Pesce, Arvada, Colorado; Design Pamela Frye, Denver, Colorado) font: Berkley Book; cruise clip art: Dover Publications

page 70 Kelton at 14 Months
Color Box ink: Clearsnap; decorative scissors: Fiskars

page 72 Recipes for an "oh Joshuuuaaa" moment
Fonts and clip art: Print Artist by Sierra; paint stickers: Stickopotamus; cooking stickers: The Gifted Line

page 73 Doug & Tracy
Patterned paper: Keeping Memories Alive

page 74 Rodos
Font: Creating Keepsakes from the Creative Lettering CD

page 75 Mommy Wanted
Log letters: Provo Craft; patterned paper: Provo Craft

page 76 My Wonderful Husband Andrew
Font: Bradley Hand ITC from MS Publisher; heart punch: McGill

page 77 The Christmas Thief
Green patterned paper: Club Scrap; tree paper: Liz King by EK Success; letter stickers and borders: Me & My Big Ideas; font: DJ Inkers

page 78 Once Upon A Time
Page topper: Cock-A-Doodle; border stickers: Me & My Big Ideas; decorative scissors: Fiskars, Provo Craft; font: black letter downloaded from the Internet

page 79 One Fine Day in May
Patterned paper: Colorbök

page 80 Tree Cutting at Genesee Mountain
Snowflake patterned paper: Debbie Mumm; swirl paper: Making Memories; vellum: Paper Adventures

page 81 December 2000 Calendar page
Patterned paper: Northern Spy, Keeping Memories Alive; font: source unknown; stickers: Hambly Studios, Mrs. Grossman's

page 83 Memories of Our Engagement
Patterned paper: source unknown; Victorian scissors: Fiskars; heart stencil

page 84 Mother's Day
Patterned paper: Colorbök; pansies stickers: Paper House; number stickers: Provo Craft

page 85 Letter to Meg
Patterned paper: source unknown; font: Times New Roman from MS Word; decorative scissors: Fiskars

page 86 Santa Claus Is Coming to Town
Patterned paper: Scrapbook Wizard; small music note punches: Carl; medium music note punches: EK Success; large music note punches: Marvy Uchida

page 87 The Sunday Funnies
Font: Anything Goes from Creating Keepsakes

page 88 Boxerchamp
Holographic paper: Grafix; stamp pad: Stampin' Up

page 88 Monopoly
Stickers: Mrs. Grossman's, Colorbök; sticker letters: Creative Memories

page 89 Noteworthy
Daisy punch: Family Treasures; letter stickers: Stickler Stickers

page 90 Drivers License
Sponged clouds; doll, sun and dirt mound die cuts: Stamping Station; font: Tempo from MS Word

page 90 Crime and Verdict
Patterned paper: Hot Off The Press

page 90 Wanted: Jansen Clarke Wooton
Color-copied denim and bandanna fabric on acid-free paper; decorative scissors: Fiskars

page 91 The Cat's Meow
White and black cardstock; black Pigma Micron pen: Sakura; handheld hole punch: Fiskars; lettering template: Provo Craft; black sticker letters: Creative Memories

Photo contributors

Arnott, Wendy, 91 (book jacket biography)
Charoenpap, Courtney, 77
Church of the Good Shepherd, 38
  Brothers Photography, 28 E. Huntington Dr., Arcadia, CA 91006
Johnson, Tracy, 73
Mabe, Dawn, 19
Marko, Adrienne, 81
Mieden Cox, Connie, 84
Moore, Tom, cover
  Party Crashers Photography, 5978 S. Holly St., Englewood, CO 80111
My Wonderful Husband Andrew, 76
  Stephen Lassman Studios, PO Box 33, Thornhill, Ontario L3T3N1 CANADA
Pesce, Michelle, 68
Rendon, Shawna, 26
Rueger, Lydia, 67
Socorro, Leah, 86
Steligo, Kathy, 33
Trujillo, Ken, cover

Sources

The following companies manufacture products featured in this book. Please check your local retailers to find these materials. In addition, we have made every attempt to properly credit the items mentioned in this book. We apologize to any company that we have listed incorrectly or the sources were unknown, and we would appreciate hearing from you.

3L Corp.
(800) 828-3130 (wholesale only)

3M Stationery
(800) 364-3577
www.3M.com

A.W. Cute Stickers n' Stuff
(877) 560-6943
www.awcute.com

All Night Media®, Inc.
(800) 782-6733

Amscan Inc.
(800) 444-8887

Bazzill Basics Paper
(480) 558-8557

Carl Mfg. USA, Inc.
(800) 257-4771

Clearsnap Inc.
(800) 448-4862
www.clearsnap.com

Close To My Heart®
(888) 655-6552
www.closetomyheart.com

Club Scrap™
(888) 634-9100
www.clubscrap.com

Cock-A-Doodle Design, Inc.
(800) 262 9727
www.cockadoodledesign.com

Colorbök
(800) 366-4660 (wholesale only)

Craf-T Products
(507) 235-3996

Crafts, Etc. Ltd.
(800) 888-0321

Creating Keepsakes
www.creatingkeepsakes.com

Creative Imaginations
(800) 942-6487
www.cigift.com

Creative Memories®
(800) 468-9335
www.creative-memories.com

C-Thru® Ruler Company, The
(800) 243-8419 (wholesale only)
www.cthruruler.com

Cut-It-Up™
(530) 389-2233
www.scrapamento.com

Debbie Mumm®
(888) 819-2923

Deluxe Cuts
(480) 497-9005
www.deluxecuts.com

D.J. Inkers™
(800) 325-4890

DMD Industries, Inc.
(800) 805-9890 (wholesale only)
www.dmdind.com

Dover Publications
(800) 223-3130

EK Success™
(800) 524-1349
www.eksuccess.com

Ellison® Craft and Design
(800) 253-2238
www.ellison.com

Emagination Crafts, Inc.
(630) 833-9521
ww.emaginationcrafts.com

Family Treasures, Inc.®
(800) 413-2645
www.familytreasures.com

Fiskars, Inc.
(800) 950-0203
www.fiskars.com

Frances Meyer, Inc.®
(800) 372-6237
www.francesmeyer.com

Sources (continued)

Gifted Line, The
(800) 533-7263

Grafix® Graphic Art Systems, Inc.
(800) 447-2349
www.grafixarts.com

Hallmark Cards, Inc.
(800) 425-6275

Hambly Studios
(800) 451-3999

Hot Off The Press
(800) 227-9595
www.paperpizazz.com

Impress Rubber Stamps
(206) 901-9101

Inkadinkado® Rubber Stamps
(800) 888-4652

Inspire Graphics
(877) 472-3427

Judi-Kins
(310) 515-1115

Katee's Kut-Ups
(858) 679-2132

Keeping Memories Alive™
(800) 419-4949
www.scrapbooks.com

Lion Brand Yarn
(800) 258-9276
www.lionbrand.com

Magenta Rubber Stamps
(800) 565-5254
www.magentarubberstamps.com

Making Memories
(800) 286-5263
www.makingmemories.com

Martha Stewart Living
(800) 950-7130
www.marthastewart.com

Marvy® Uchida
(800) 541-5877
www.uchida.com

Masterpiece® Studios
(800) 447-0219
www.masterpiecestudios.com

McGill Inc.
(800) 982-9884
www.mcgillinc.com

Me & My Big Ideas
(949) 589-4607 (wholesale only)
www.meandmybigideas.com

Mrs. Grossman's Paper Company
(800) 429-4549 (wholesale only)
www.mrsgrossmans.com

Northern Spy
(530) 620-7430
www.northernspy.com

NRN Designs
(800) 421-6958 (wholesale only)
www.nrndesigns.com

Paper Adventures®
(800) 727-0699 (wholesale only)
www.paperadventures.com

Paper House Productions
(800) 255-7316
www.paperhouseproductions.com

Paper Patch®, The
(801) 253-3018 (wholesale only)
www.paperpatch.com

Posh Impressions
(800) 421-7674

Provo Craft®
(888) 577-3545 (wholesale only)
www.provocraft.com

PSX Design™
(800) 782-6748

R.A. Lang
(800) 648-2388

Rubber Stampede
(800) 423-4135

Sakura of America
(800) 776-6257
www.gellyroll.com

Scrapbook Wizard™, The
(801) 947-0019 (wholesale only)
www.scrapbookwizard.com

Scrap-Ease®
(800) 642-6762 (wholesale only)
www.E-Craftshop.com

Scrap Pagerz™
(425) 645-0696
www.scrappagerz.com

Scrappin' Dreams
(417) 831-1882 (wholesale only)
www.scrappindreams.com

SEI, Inc.
(800) 333-3279

Sierra On-Line, Inc.
(800) 757-7707
www.sierrahome.com

Stamp Doctor, The
www.stampdoctor.com

Stampendous®/Mark Enterprises
(800) 869-0474
www.stampendous.com

Stampin' Up!®
(800) 782-6787
www.stampinup.com

Stamping Station Inc.
(801) 444-3828
www.stampingstation.com

Stamps "N" Memories
(909) 381-6063

Stickopotamus®
(888) 270-4443 (wholesale only)
www.stickopotamus.com

TooMuchFun Rubberstamps
(800) 351-1863

Westrim® Crafts
(800) 727-2727 (wholesale only)
www.westrimcrafts.com

Wübie Prints
(888) 256-0107
www.wubieprints.com

Bibliography

Ernst, Janet. *Power Penmanship: An Illustrated Guide to Enhancing Your Image Through the Art of Handwriting Style.* 1993. New York: William Morrow and Company.

Getty, Barbara and Inga Dubay. *Write Now: A Complete Self-Teaching Program for Better Handwriting.* 1991. Portland, Oregon: Continuing Education Press; Portland State University.

Index

About me memory prompts, 25
Acrostic journaling, 76
Active words, using, 30-31
Adding journaling to finished pages, 64-65
Being a photo detective, 15
Beyond the basics, 26-51
Book jacket biography, 91
Bullet journaling, 70
Calendar journaling, 81
Children memory prompts, 23
Classified ad journaling, 75
Comic strip journaling, 87
Correspondence journaling, 85
Credits and sources, 94-96
Descriptive words, using, 28-29
Dictionary journaling, 71
Fairy tale journaling, 78
Fixing journaling mistakes, 67
Found journaling, 80
Gallery of other styles of journaling, 88-91
Getting Started, 12-25
Grammar guide, 93
Handwriting, tips for improving, 66
Heritage memory prompts, 24
Information every page should include, 18
Interviewing tips, 41
Introduction, 7
Journaling about the photos you
   don't have, 62-63
Just write, 17
Leaving room for journaling, 19
List, acton words, 31
List, descriptive words, 29
List, sense words, 35
Making a memory wheel, 92
Making design and journaling
   work together, 44-51
Newspaper journaling, 82
Other voices, incorporating, 40
Perspective journaling, 83
Poetic journaling, 79
Postcard journaling, 74
Rebus journaling, 86
Recipe journaling, 72
Senses, appealing to, 32-35
Spending time with your photos, 14
Step-by-step journaling, 77
Think outside the box: other styles, 68-91
Thoughts and feelings, incorporating, 36-39
Timeline journaling, 73
Tips for improving your handwriting, 66
Tools to help you journal, 42-43
Top-ten journaling, 84
Travel memory prompts, 21
Wedding memory prompts, 22
What is journaling?, 8
When journaling is difficult, 52-67
When you absolutely have to journal, 20-25
   about me memory prompts, 25
   children memory prompts, 23
   heritage memory prompts, 24
   travel memory prompts, 21
   wedding memory prompts, 22
Why you may not journal (yet), 9
Why you should journal, 10-11
Writer's block, overcoming, 54-57
Writing about the hard times, 58-61